ACORN SAFETY SERVICES

Logistics & Warehousing: Health & Safety Leadership

Streamline Operations, Ensure Safety, and Boost Compliance

Copyright © 2024 by Acorn Safety Services

©2024 Acorn Safety Services Ltd. All rights reserved. No part of this publication may be reproduced, distributed, or transmitted in any form or by any means, including photocopying, recording, or other electronic or mechanical methods, without the prior written permission of the publisher, except in the case of brief quotations embodied in critical reviews and certain other noncommercial uses permitted by copyright law.

The information provided in this book, "Logistics & Warehousing: Health & Safety Leadership (Streamline Operations, Ensure Safety, and Boost Compliance)" is for general informational purposes only. The views and opinions expressed in this book are those of the authors and do not necessarily reflect the official policy or position of Acorn Safety Services Ltd or any associated entity or individual.

Acorn Safety Services Ltd and the authors make no representations or warranties of any kind, express or implied, about the completeness, accuracy, reliability, suitability, or availability with respect to the book or the information, products, services, or related graphics contained in the book for any purpose. Any reliance you place on such information is therefore strictly at your own risk.

In no event will Acorn Safety Services Ltd or the authors be liable for any loss or damage including without limitation, indirect or consequential loss or damage, or any loss or damage whatsoever arising from loss of data or profits arising out of, or in connection with, the use of this book.

The advice and strategies contained herein may not be suitable for your situation. You should consult with a professional where appropriate. Acorn Safety Services Ltd is not responsible for any financial claims or any outcomes resulting from the implementation of strategies discussed in this book.

Contents

Foreword		iv
Preface		viii
1	Decoding The Essentials: Understanding Health and Safety Law...	1
2	Mastering Risk Management in Warehousing	12
3	Optimising Safety in Logistics Operations	23
4	Cultivating A Safety Culture	34
5	Technological Innovations Enhancing Safety	45
6	Navigating Health and Safety Training	56
7	Health and Safety in the Transport Yard Environment	66
8	Legal Compliance and Beyond	77
9	Health and Safety Metrics and Reporting	88
10	Integrating Health and Safety with Business Strategy	99
11	Leveraging Health and Safety Consultancy for Strategic...	110
12	Examples from the Field: Success Stories in Health and...	120
13	Acorn Compliance Antidote©	126
Embracing The Future: a Call to Action for Continued Safety...		136
Other Titles Available From Amazon		139
Still Looking to Remove Your Problems?		140

Foreword

Hi, I'm grateful you took the opportunity to get this book. Over the decades, Acorn Safety Services consultants have dedicated their careers to mastering the intricacies of Health and Safety Consultancy. With over 100 years of combined experience, we've encountered countless misconceptions and fielded numerous questions about the industry. This motivated us to compile this much publicised book to dispel myths and guide you through the complexities of health and safety compliance in the logistics and warehousing sector.

After all, maybe you've tried to navigate the labyrinth of legal requirements and found the constantly changing regulations overwhelming. Keeping up-to-date while managing day-to-day operations can seem like juggling while blindfolded—a daunting task that leaves many feeling unsure and unprotected.

Maybe you've also faced the challenge of training your team adequately, ensuring every member not only understands the safety protocols but also diligently follows them. It's frustrating when despite your best efforts, gaps in compliance emerge, threatening both safety and operational efficiency.

Or maybe you've even encountered resistance from within your own ranks—team members who view safety measures as unnecessary red tape, slowing down operations without appreciating the protective buffer they provide against accidents and legal actions.

And look, I get it, it's not fair.

The truth is, you're not alone. It seems most senior managers and directors in the logistics and warehousing sector in the UK are becoming victims of these very issues, struggling to keep their head above water in the sea of compliance requirements.

That feeling of frustration, isolation, and constant pressure isn't just a personal burden—it's a shared challenge across the industry. It gnaws at you, night and day, as you strive to safeguard your operations, protect your team, and satisfy regulatory bodies.

Here's what most don't realise: the true cost of non-compliance goes beyond fines and legal fees. It seeps into every aspect of your business, eroding trust, endangering lives, and undermining the very foundations of your operational integrity.

And now with the possibility of more stringent regulations on the horizon, the landscape of logistics and warehousing is becoming even more daunting. If you're not ahead of the curve, you're not just static; you're sliding backwards.

It seems most are left in a state of perpetual anxiety, caught in a cycle of reactive measures rather than proactive strategies. The fear of significant incidents, the potential for severe financial losses, and the nightmare of reputational damage—it's a trifecta of threats that no industry leader should navigate alone.

The Compliance Carousel

Navigating the tumultuous landscape of health and safety compliance in logistics and warehousing is akin to an endless ride on a carousel—a Compliance Carousel. This carousel spins relentlessly, pulling senior managers and directors in UK logistics and warehousing into a cyclical journey of frustration and false hope. In this chapter, we will dissect each phase of this perpetual loop, revealing the hidden pitfalls and challenges that keep you from reaching true compliance and operational peace.

Trigger Alert

Perhaps you've recently faced a near-miss incident or an audit that didn't go as smoothly as anticipated. The immediate reaction is a rush of urgency to tighten protocols and ensure no stone is left unturned in compliance. This trigger not only heightens your awareness but also sets you on high alert for potential liabilities and risks lurking in your operations. The anxiety of facing hefty fines or, worse, operational shutdown, propels you into action, initiating a series of steps aimed at rectifying perceived shortcomings.

Overhaul Overdrive

Driven by the initial panic, you might dive headfirst into overhauling your current systems. It's a flurry of activity: updating safety procedures, training employees, and perhaps investing in new safety equipment. On the surface, it feels proactive and decisive. Meetings are held, workshops conducted, and memos circulated. Yet, the focus tends to lean heavily on immediate fixes rather than addressing underlying systemic issues. The surface-level changes create a deceptive veneer of compliance, but without digging deeper, the foundation remains shaky.

Compliance Complacency

With the new changes seemingly in place, there's a brief sigh of relief. You might believe that the adjustments are sufficient. Audits are passed—barely but passed nonetheless—and the immediate fear of legal repercussions begins to wane. This complacency is dangerous; it masks the need for continuous improvement and embeds a false sense of security. The underlying issues continue to fester, unnoticed or perhaps conveniently ignored, given the apparent calm.

Audit Anxiety

Then comes the announcement of an upcoming audit, and the cycle's intensity ramps up. Perhaps you scramble to ensure that everything is in tip-top shape, running last-minute checks and refreshers on the new systems implemented. The audit looms large, a stark reminder of the potential weaknesses that might be unearthed. This stage is fraught with tension, as you hope that the cosmetic fixes hold up under scrutiny.

False Dawn

Post-audit, perhaps the results are better than expected. There's celebration and a collective breath of relief—finally, it seems like you've turned a corner. But as time passes, small cracks begin to appear. Maybe an employee bypasses a new procedure because it's cumbersome, or a piece of safety equipment fails. Slowly, the realisation dawns that the cycle hasn't been broken; it's merely paused. And soon, you find yourself back at the trigger alert, with another incident or audit failure, and the sinking feeling that nothing has truly changed.

It just goes to show, you would be wise to do something different to achieve full compliance in all health and safety elements and stop the pain and frustration.

Which is why I'm glad you're reading this book, because as you turn the page and start reading, you will finally get the answers and insight that you're looking for.

Preface

Imagine a world where your logistics and warehousing operations run with the precision of a Swiss watch—where safety is not just a compliance checkbox but the backbone of your business, ensuring smooth operations, protecting your workforce, and enhancing your bottom line. In the bustling, dynamic field of logistics and warehousing, the complexity of operations often leads to a focus on immediate issues: meeting delivery deadlines, maintaining inventory accuracy, and managing costs. However, the core of truly transformative leadership in this sector lies in something seemingly less immediate but far more critical—health, safety, and compliance.

In this competitive landscape, the role of a senior manager or director is not just to manage, but to lead with vision and foresight. You are tasked not only with keeping the wheels of commerce turning but doing so in a way that safeguards the health and well-being of every employee under your watch. This is no small feat. It requires a robust understanding of the laws that govern your operations, an innovative approach to risk management, and a strategic mindset that aligns safety with overall business objectives.

The first part of leading effectively is understanding the stakes. In the UK, logistics and warehousing are not just crucial economic sectors; they are environments where the risk of accidents and injuries is significant. From forklift operations in tight spaces to the management of hazardous materials, every square foot of your facility must be a testament to safety and efficiency. This isn't just about meeting legal requirements—it's about building systems that encourage productivity and morale, creating a workplace where employees feel secure and valued.

Moreover, the landscape of health and safety is not static. New regulations, technological advancements, and changing economic conditions continuously reshape the terrain. Staying ahead means not only keeping abreast of these changes but being able to anticipate and react to them before they become challenges. This proactive approach transforms safety and compliance from a cost centre into a strategic asset—a tool for gaining a competitive advantage and achieving market leadership.

The second part of this leadership journey is mastering the tools at your disposal. This includes cutting-edge technologies that enhance safety and efficiency, the development of a risk management framework that protects your operations from unexpected disruptions, and the cultivation of a safety culture that permeates every level of your organisation. It's about seeing safety and compliance not as regulatory burdens but as opportunities to excel and set your operations apart from the competition.

In embracing these tools, you will find that they are not just protective measures. They are also instruments of efficiency and quality, reducing downtime, enhancing employee satisfaction, and improving customer trust. They provide data and insights that enable you to make informed decisions quickly, adapt to changes in the marketplace, and continually refine your operations to maintain a competitive edge.

Finally, the third part is about integration. This is where safety and health management cease to be siloed aspects of your operation and become integral to your strategic business objectives. It's about aligning every safety protocol, every piece of compliance legislation, and every risk management initiative with your broader business goals. Whether it's reducing costs, enhancing brand reputation, or entering new markets, health and safety management can be a lever for growth and innovation.

Integrating these elements requires not just skill and knowledge, but a change in perspective. It requires seeing yourself not just as a manager of resources but as a leader of people. It calls for a commitment to excellence and a dedication to the well-being of every individual who contributes to your success. This is leadership in logistics and warehousing at its most profound and impactful.

As you embark on this journey through the chapters of this book, you will discover ways to streamline operations, boost compliance, and ensure safety in a manner that is both innovative and practical. Each chapter will equip you with the knowledge and tools to not just meet the standards set before you but to exceed them, setting new benchmarks for excellence in your field.

The transformation starts here. It starts with you. Embrace this opportunity to redefine what it means to lead in logistics and warehousing, to take your operations to new heights, and to become a benchmark for excellence in an industry that is the backbone of our economy.

1

Decoding The Essentials: Understanding Health and Safety Law In Logistics

"Safety isn't expensive, it's priceless." — Unknown

Introduction to Health and Safety Legislation

Navigating the labyrinth of health and safety legislation in the UK isn't just about compliance; it's a crucial component of leadership in logistics and warehousing. Understanding the framework not only shields your operation from legal repercussions but also fortifies the backbone of your business—its people.

Overview of UK Health and Safety Laws

At the heart of UK health and safety legislation is the Health and Safety at Work etc. Act 1974. This foundational act sets out the general duties which employers have towards employees and members of the public, and employees have to themselves and each other. These laws are applicable to all work sectors, but for you in logistics and warehousing, they hold particular significance due to the high-risk nature of activities involved from manual handling to operating heavy machinery.

Beyond the 1974 Act, regulations like the Management of Health and Safety at Work Regulations 1999 build upon these foundations, requiring you to actively manage and assess workplace risks. Similarly, the Workplace (Health, Safety and Welfare) Regulations 1992 cover a range of basics from suitable lighting and ventilation to safety equipment and floor conditions.

In logistics, where the movement and storage of goods are central, specific regulations such as the Manual Handling Operations Regulations 1992 and the Provision and Use of Work Equipment Regulations 1998 are particularly relevant. These laws mandate the need for risk assessment and appropriate control measures to manage the risks associated with workplace equipment and manual handling tasks.

Key Legal Responsibilities for Employers

As a senior manager or director, your legal responsibilities are both broad and specific. Primarily, you must ensure, as far as reasonably practicable, the health, safety, and welfare of all your employees. This includes creating and maintaining a safe working environment and providing adequate training and information.

Risk management should be a continuous activity. Implementing systematic health and safety management involves not only adherence to the laws but embracing a culture that prioritises safety. You must conduct risk assessments to identify potential hazards and implement practical measures to mitigate these risks. Documentation is key here—not just for compliance, but as a tool for ongoing improvement. Regularly revising risk assessments ensures they remain relevant and effective in mitigating risks in your ever-evolving operational environment.

In addition, encouraging open lines of communication is crucial. This involves not only informing staff about the risks and the measures in place to manage them but also training them adequately so they understand their roles in maintaining workplace safety. Furthermore, consultation with employees on matters affecting their health and safety is not just a legal requirement, but a practical way to enhance safety measures and involve employees in the conversation about their work environment.

The Role of Health and Safety Executive (HSE)

The Health and Safety Executive (HSE) is the national independent watchdog for work-related health, safety, and illness. It acts in the public interest to reduce work-related death and serious injury across the UK's workplaces. For you, understanding the role of HSE is pivotal in ensuring your operations align with legal standards and best practices.

HSE not only enforces health and safety law but also provides guidance, advice, and support to help you manage health and safety effectively. From detailed guides on specific regulations to broad advice on risk management practices, HSE resources can be invaluable in helping you design, implement, and oversee your health and safety protocols.

Moreover, HSE's oversight extends to on-site inspections and investigations, which means it's crucial that your operations consistently comply with the law. Non-compliance can result in legal action from HSE, including fines and, in severe cases, prosecution. More than ever, in the logistics and warehousing sector, where operations are highly scrutinised for safety compliance, understanding and cooperating with HSE can substantially mitigate legal risks and enhance operational safety.

Navigating UK health and safety laws may seem daunting, but with a robust understanding and strategic implementation of these regulations, you can ensure not only legal compliance but also a safer, more efficient working environment for your team. By integrating these legal requirements into your operational ethos, you contribute significantly to safeguarding the well-being of your employees and the productivity of your operations. Remember, effective health and safety management is as much about encouraging a culture of continuous improvement and accountability as it is about compliance.

Risk Assessment Fundamentals

Identifying Hazards

In the bustling world of logistics and warehousing, the first step towards safeguarding your operations is identifying potential hazards. This process forms the bedrock of your risk management strategy and is pivotal in creating a safe working environment for your team. So, let's dive into the nuts and bolts of how you can spot these hazards effectively.

Hazards in a logistics and warehousing environment can broadly fall into several categories such as physical, chemical, biological, ergonomic, and psychosocial. Each category comes with its own set of challenges. For instance, physical hazards might include things like forklift operations, manual handling, or slips, trips, and falls due to uneven or slippery surfaces. Chemical hazards could involve exposure to harmful substances like fuels, solvents, or cleaning agents.

The process of identifying these hazards typically involves a combination of several proactive and reactive techniques. Walk-through surveys, staff consultations, and examining accident and ill-health records are crucial. Engaging with your employees can provide firsthand insights into potential risks and the effectiveness of existing control measures.

Moreover, staying updated with industry trends and case studies can also shed light on emerging risks that might not have been previously considered. For example, the rapid increase in automation and use of robotics in warehouses might introduce new hazards related to the interaction between humans and machines.

Remember, the goal here is not just to tick a compliance box but to gain a thorough understanding of all potential risks in your work environment. This comprehensive approach ensures that no stone is left unturned, keeping your operations smooth and your team safe.

Assessing Risks

Once you have identified the potential hazards, the next step is to assess the level of risk associated with each hazard. This risk assessment is crucial in determining how severe a hazard could be and therefore, how urgently it needs to be addressed.

The assessment process should consider both the likelihood of the hazard leading to an injury or health issue and the severity of the outcome if it were to occur. For example, the risk of someone falling from a height in your warehouse might be low if measures are already in place, but the severity of an injury from such a fall could be high, warranting stringent controls.

A practical approach to risk assessment in a logistics setting involves prioritising risks using a risk matrix. This tool helps you categorise risks based on their severity and likelihood, making it easier to see which ones need more immediate attention. This prioritisation helps in allocating resources more effectively, ensuring that the most significant risks are mitigated first.

Furthermore, it's crucial to involve team members in this process. They often have valuable insights into the practicalities of their work environment that might not be immediately obvious from a management perspective. Their input can make your risk assessments more accurate and grounded in the reality of daily operations.

Implementing Control Measures

After identifying and assessing the risks, the focus shifts to implementing control measures. These measures are your first line of defence against potential hazards in your warehouse or logistics operation and are crucial in mitigating risks.

When deciding on control measures, the hierarchy of control provides a proven framework. This starts with eliminating the hazard entirely, which is the most effective control. If elimination isn't possible, substitution with a less hazardous option, engineering controls, and administrative controls follow, in that order. Lastly, if other controls cannot reduce the risk alone, personal protective equipment (PPE) should be used as a last resort.

For instance, if manual handling is identified as a risk, could automation or mechanical aids eliminate the need for manual lifting? If not, could changes to the task layout or schedule reduce the frequency and strain of these activities? Training and clear procedural guidelines can also play a significant role in risk mitigation, ensuring everyone understands how to manage risks effectively.

Regularly reviewing and updating these controls is equally important. The dynamic nature of logistics and warehousing means new technologies, processes, and regulations are continually emerging. Ensuring that your control measures are up to date is crucial for maintaining a safe working environment.

Moreover, documenting all aspects of your risk assessment process is not only a legal requirement but also a practical tool for ongoing management. This documentation should be accessible and understandable, providing clear guidance for all employees and forming the basis for training and induction programs.

In conclusion, mastering these fundamentals of risk assessment not only ensures compliance with health and safety laws but also enhances the efficiency and productivity of your operations. By systematically identifying hazards, assessing the associated risks, and implementing effective controls, you equip your business to thrive in a competitive and challenging industry landscape.

Employee Rights and Responsibilities

Worker Participation in Safety

In the dynamic world of logistics and warehousing, the safety of your workforce isn't just a regulatory requirement; it's a core element of your operational success. Encouraging active participation from your employees in safety procedures isn't merely about compliance—it's about creating a culture of mutual responsibility and proactive safety management.

Worker participation means involving your team in every step of the safety process, from the identification of hazards to the development and review of safety policies. It's crucial that you, as a senior manager or director, encourage an environment where every employee feels empowered and responsible for not only their safety but also the safety of their colleagues.

Start by setting up safety committees or appointing safety representatives among the workforce, especially those directly engaged in high-risk operations. These roles are not just about fulfilling a legal quota; they're about giving your teams a voice. Safety committees should meet regularly and be given the real power to make recommendations for safety improvements.

Another effective strategy is to implement suggestion schemes, where employees can anonymously submit their safety concerns or improvement ideas. This can be particularly empowering for workers who might otherwise be hesitant to speak up. Regular town hall meetings can also be an excellent forum for discussing safety issues, enabling a transparent dialogue between management and staff.

Remember, the key here is not just to listen but to act. When employees see their input leading to real changes, it reinforces their value within the company, bolsters morale, and, crucially, enhances compliance with safety protocols.

Training Requirements

Training is the backbone of safety in logistics and warehousing. It's not just about ticking a box; it's about building a skilled, aware, and competent workforce. As a leader in this sector, it is your duty to ensure that every employee not only understands the specific risks associated with their job but also how to manage these risks effectively.

Training should be regular, comprehensive, and tailored to the particular needs of your operations and workforce. This includes not only induction training for new employees but also ongoing training for all staff. The landscape of logistics and warehousing is continually evolving, with new technologies and methods being developed. Your safety training programs should evolve accordingly.

Consider different training methods to suit various learning styles and roles within your company. Interactive workshops, hands-on simulations, and e-learning modules are all effective ways to engage different types of learners. Also, think beyond traditional safety training—include leadership training for middle managers and team leaders to ensure they are equipped to uphold safety standards within their teams.

Crucially, training should also cover what employees should do in case of an emergency. Emergency drills should be conducted regularly—not just as a formality but as a practical, engaging learning experience that tests the real-world application of training.

Reporting and Rectifying Issues

A crucial pillar of maintaining a safe workplace is the procedure for reporting and rectifying issues. As a leader, it's your responsibility to establish and maintain an effective system for this. Employees must feel comfortable and supported in reporting safety issues without fear of reprisal.

Firstly, ensure that there are clear, simple channels for reporting safety concerns. This could be through direct line managers, safety representatives, or through an anonymous reporting system. Technology can be a great facilitator here; consider implementing a digital tool that allows employees to report issues quickly and easily.

Once an issue is reported, the response must be swift and effective. This is where your established risk assessment procedures come into play. Each reported issue should be assessed promptly to determine its severity and the speed with which it needs to be addressed. Regular feedback to the person who reported the issue is essential, as it demonstrates that their concerns are being taken seriously and handled appropriately.

Moreover, don't just stop at addressing the immediate issue. Analyse the root cause to understand why the problem occurred in the first place and what can be done to prevent it in the future. This might involve revisiting your risk assessments, training programs, or even the overall safety culture within your organisation.

In conclusion, remember that the rights and responsibilities of your employees are not just items on a checklist. They are integral components of your operational strategy that can drive not just compliance but also efficiency, morale, and ultimately the success of your logistics or warehousing business. By encouraging a culture of safety that actively involves everyone from the ground up, you not only comply with the law—you create a safer, more productive workplace.

RECAP AND ACTION ITEMS

You've just navigated through the crucial aspects of health and safety law in the logistics sector, covering everything from the overarching legislation to specific employee rights and responsibilities. As you steer your operations towards compliance and safety excellence, it's vital to keep these insights at the forefront of your strategy.

Firstly, it's essential to maintain a crystal-clear understanding of the UK's health and safety laws. Remember, these are not just guidelines but mandates that safeguard both your employees and your business. Regularly revisiting the Health and Safety at Work etc. Act 1974, along with the latest updates from the Health and Safety Executive (HSE), will keep you well-informed and compliant.

Now, let's talk action. Begin by conducting a comprehensive review of your current risk assessment processes. Are you thoroughly identifying all potential hazards within your operations? When assessing risks, consider the long-term implications of your findings. It's not just about compliance; it's about encouraging a safe work environment that enhances productivity and employee morale.

Implementing control measures is your next critical step. This isn't a one-off task but an ongoing process that adapts to new challenges and changes within your sector. Ensure these measures are practical, clearly communicated, and fully integrated into your daily operations.

Moreover, empowering your employees is key to reinforcing a culture of safety. This means actively involving them in safety discussions, providing continuous training, and ensuring they are aware of their rights and responsibilities. Encourage open communication, where employees feel safe to report hazards without fear of reprisal.

Finally, set up a regular audit and review schedule to assess the effectiveness of your safety protocols. Adjustments might be necessary as your business grows and evolves or as new legislation comes into effect.

By taking these steps, you not only comply with the law but also position your business as a leader in operational safety and efficiency. Remember, a safe workplace is a productive workplace. So, let's get moving—your leadership in this arena not only sets industry standards but also solidifies the foundation of your company's success.

2

Mastering Risk Management in Warehousing

"It is not the strongest of the species that survive, nor the most intelligent, but the one most responsive to change." - Charles Darwin

Managing Warehouse Risks

Navigating the labyrinth of warehouse management, you're bound to encounter a few dragons. From towering stacks of inventory threatening to topple over to the ever-present danger of equipment mishaps, the risks are as varied as they are daunting. But fear not! By mastering a few key strategies, you can turn these potential pitfalls into mere stepping stones on your path to operational excellence. Let's delve into the essentials of managing warehouse risks, covering everything from common hazards to equipment safety, and ensuring your warehouse is a bastion of productivity and safety.

Common Warehouse Hazards

First up, let's tackle the common warehouse hazards. Every warehouse, regardless of size or function, faces a set of core risks. These typically include slips, trips, and falls, manual handling injuries, and impacts from moving vehicles. It's not just about avoiding accidents; it's about creating an environment where safety is as automatic as breathing.

Slips, trips, and falls might sound trivial, but they account for a significant portion of workplace injuries. The key here is housekeeping. Ensure all aisles and passageways are clear of debris and promptly clean up any spills. Adequate lighting and proper floor markings also go a long way in guiding staff safely around the premises.

Manual handling is another critical area. It's not just about lifting techniques; it's about understanding and organising the workflow to minimise the need for manual lifting altogether. Consider the layout of your warehouse and the flow of goods. Are there points where unnecessary lifting occurs? Can these be minimised by using more appropriate machinery or adjusting the layout?

Lastly, vehicles—whether fork-lifts or pallet trucks—are indispensable but bring their own set of risks. Ensuring that all drivers are properly trained and that vehicles are regularly maintained is just the start. Implementing strict traffic management plans can prevent a lot of heartache. This means designated pedestrian and vehicle routes, clear signage, and perhaps even physical barriers where necessary.

Safe Storage Practices

On to the backbone of any warehouse operation: storage. It's not just about stacking boxes. Effective storage practices are crucial for both safety and efficiency. The goal? To store goods in a way that minimises risk and maximises accessibility.

Start with the layout. The arrangement of your racks and shelves should facilitate smooth operations, with frequently used items easily accessible. Ensure that all storage units are robust and suitable for the types of goods you're storing. Regular inspections are a must to check for any signs of damage or wear and tear.

Weight limits should be religiously adhered to. Overloading not only poses a risk to staff but can also damage your goods and shelving units. Similarly, ensure that items are evenly distributed and securely placed to prevent any adventurous rolls or shifts.

Fire risk is also a significant concern with storage. Combustible materials need to be identified and stored with special care, ideally away from main traffic areas and in flame-resistant containers. Regular fire safety audits can help identify potential risks before they flare up into real problems.

Equipment Safety

Finally, let's talk equipment. In a world where time is money, and downtime is the enemy, keeping your equipment in top shape is non-negotiable. This isn't just about maintaining productivity; it's about ensuring the safety of every person who steps into your warehouse.

Routine maintenance checks are the cornerstone of equipment safety. This means not only fixing issues as they arise but actively looking for potential problems before they become serious. Implement a regular maintenance schedule, and stick to it religiously. Ensure that all equipment operators are trained to spot warning signs of malfunction.

Training, in general, is a critical component of equipment safety. Every operator should be thoroughly trained not just in how to use the equipment, but in how to use it safely. This includes understanding the limits of each machine, knowing how to respond in an emergency, and being aware of their responsibilities under health and safety legislation.

Moreover, consider the ergonomic design of the equipment. Prolonged use of poorly designed machinery can lead to a host of musculoskeletal issues. Invest in equipment that not only gets the job done but supports the well-being of your staff.

By weaving these strands together—awareness of hazards, safe storage practices, and rigorous equipment safety—you're not just preventing accidents. You're building a culture of safety that can significantly enhance operational efficiency and staff morale. Remember, a safe warehouse is a productive warehouse.

Emergency Preparedness

When the unexpected hits, the difference between a minor hiccup and a full-blown catastrophe in your warehouse can often boil down to one thing: your level of preparedness. Let's deep dive into the essentials of emergency preparedness, ensuring you're not just reacting to emergencies, but preemptively managing them.

Emergency Plan Development

First things first, developing a robust emergency plan is your frontline defence against potential disasters. Think of it as the blueprint that keeps your operations running smoothly when chaos looms. This plan shouldn't be a dusty file sitting on a shelf; it needs to be a dynamic, well-practised procedure.

Start by identifying all potential emergencies that could impact your warehouse. These could range from fires and floods to cyber-attacks or even pandemics. Involve your team in these brainstorming sessions. Often, the insights from someone on the ground can be incredibly valuable and might highlight risks that aren't immediately obvious from the management suite.

Once you've mapped out the threats, it's time to develop response strategies for each scenario. This involves outlining specific roles and responsibilities—know who does what when alarms go off. Ensure that there's a clear chain of command and that everyone knows who they report to in an emergency.

Communication is your ally here. Establish how you'll communicate with your team during an emergency. Will you use intercoms, mobiles, or perhaps a specialised alert system? Whatever you choose, ensure redundancy. Technology can fail, and having a backup method can save the day.

Regular drills are a must. They keep the team's skills sharp and help identify any chinks in your emergency response armour. After each drill, gather feedback and make necessary adjustments. This iterative process can turn a good plan into a great one.

Fire Safety Management

No conversation about warehouse emergencies is complete without focusing on fire safety. Fires are a prevalent hazard and can escalate quickly, causing significant damage to life, property, and your business reputation.

Your fire safety strategy starts with risk assessment. Identify sources of ignition, fuel, and oxygen in your warehouse. Store flammable materials securely and away from direct sources of heat. Regularly inspect electrical equipment and wiring, and maintain machinery to prevent overheating and friction sparks.

Installing and maintaining proper fire suppression systems like sprinklers and extinguishers is crucial. But, it's not just about having these systems in place; it's about ensuring they are accessible and functional. Conduct regular checks and services, and replace any equipment that no longer meets safety standards.

Training your staff on fire safety is equally important. They should know how to use fire extinguishers, recognise different types of fires, and understand which extinguisher to use depending on the fire source. Regular fire drills will engrain these practices in your team's mind, making them second nature.

Lastly, keep clear and visible signage in your warehouse. Fire exit signs and evacuation maps can guide staff to safety in an emergency, potentially saving lives.

Accident Response Strategies

Despite the best laid plans, accidents can still happen. How you respond can mean the difference between a contained incident and a full-scale emergency.

First up, ensure you have a well-equipped first aid station and that staff are trained in basic first aid procedures. Knowing how to address minor injuries can prevent them from becoming major ones. For more significant incidents, having a clear procedure for summoning medical assistance quickly is vital.

Documentation is your friend when it comes to managing accidents. Implement a system for reporting and recording incidents as they happen. This not only helps in treating any injuries more effectively but also aids in investigating what went wrong and why.

Use these incident reports to tweak your risk assessments and emergency responses. Sometimes, an accident can expose flaws in your current plans that, once addressed, can significantly enhance safety.

Lastly, support from management is crucial in effective accident response. Ensure your team knows that their safety is your priority. This encourages a culture of safety and compliance where team members are more likely to report risks and adhere to safety protocols without fear of reprisal.

By weaving these threads together—robust emergency planning, stringent fire safety measures, and proactive accident response strategies—you create a tapestry of preparedness that can significantly mitigate risks in your warehouse. Remember, the goal is to be so prepared that you rarely need to put these plans into action. But should that day come, you and your team will be ready, not just to respond, but to manage the situation effectively, ensuring safety, continuity, and compliance.

Health Surveillance and Monitoring

Health Checks

In the fast-paced world of logistics and warehousing, ensuring the health of your workforce isn't just a duty; it's a strategic imperative. Regular health checks are vital in detecting potential health issues before they escalate into serious problems that could impact productivity and safety.

Initiating a comprehensive health check programme involves several key steps. First, you must understand the specific health risks associated with your particular warehouse environment. This includes factors like the handling of hazardous materials, the physical demands placed on workers, and even the mental stress associated with high-paced decision-making.

Once these risks are identified, develop a health check protocol that includes both routine screenings and targeted checks. Routine screenings might include annual physical exams, vision tests, and hearing assessments, relevant to all employees. Targeted checks, on the other hand, should address specific risks identified in your risk assessment phase. For example, if workers are frequently exposed to high noise levels, regular hearing tests should be mandated.

It's also essential to partner with healthcare professionals who can provide these checks, ensuring they have experience with occupational health. Furthermore, results from these checks should be meticulously documented and reviewed regularly to identify trends or recurring issues.

Remember, the aim here is proactive intervention. By catching potential health issues early, you not only safeguard your employees' health and improve their productivity but also reduce absenteeism and mitigate potential compensation claims.

Exposure Monitoring

Exposure monitoring is your radar for detecting invisible threats in your warehouse environment. This part of health surveillance focuses on assessing and managing the levels of exposure to harmful substances or stressful conditions at work.

Implementing an effective exposure monitoring system involves several critical actions. Foremost, you need to identify what contaminants or stress factors are present in your warehouse. These can range from airborne substances, like dust or fumes, to ergonomic risks from repetitive strain.

Once these hazards are identified, it's crucial to determine the exposure limits and compare them against the standards set by health and safety regulations. Utilising both direct reading instruments and laboratory analysis, you can gather data on the presence and concentration of these hazards.

Continuous monitoring technology can also play a pivotal role here. Devices that track air quality or noise levels in real time can provide immediate data, allowing for swift action if levels spike unexpectedly. Additionally, wearable technology can monitor individual exposure, providing a more personalised health safeguarding approach.

Your strategy should include regular reviews of monitoring equipment and procedures to ensure they remain effective and compliant with current regulations. This ongoing process not only helps in maintaining a safe working environment but also demonstrates your commitment to your team's health, boosting morale and trust within your workforce.

Occupational Illness Prevention

Preventing occupational illness is the ultimate goal of your health surveillance and monitoring strategy. This proactive approach not only helps in maintaining a healthy workforce but also reinforces your company's reputation as a responsible employer.

The first step in preventing occupational illnesses is education. Workers need to be aware of the potential health risks associated with their jobs and how they can mitigate these risks. Training sessions should be conducted regularly, not just as an onboarding procedure but as an ongoing educational effort. These sessions should cover proper use of personal protective equipment (PPE), correct handling techniques for hazardous materials, and the importance of adhering to safety protocols.

Next, encouraging a culture of openness and responsiveness is crucial. Encourage your employees to report symptoms or concerns about health issues, however minor they may seem. Early detection is key in preventing many occupational illnesses that develop over time.

Additionally, adapt your workplace ergonomics to fit the needs of your employees rather than forcing them to adapt to suboptimal working conditions. This can include adjustable workstations, appropriate lifting equipment, and sufficient rest breaks to reduce physical strain.

Lastly, consider the mental health of your employees. Stress, anxiety, and burnout can lead to serious physical health issues if left unchecked. Support programmes such as counselling services, stress management workshops, and a supportive managerial approach can make a significant difference in preventing stress-related illnesses.

By integrating these strategies into your daily operations, you create a safer, healthier workplace that not only meets regulatory standards but also supports your employees in every aspect of their health, ultimately leading to a more productive and committed workforce.

In conclusion, health surveillance and monitoring in the warehousing sector is a critical component of risk management. By implementing thorough health checks, rigorous exposure monitoring, and robust occupational illness prevention strategies, you not only safeguard the well-being of your workforce but also enhance operational efficiency and maintain compliance with health and safety regulations. Remember, a healthy workforce is a productive one, and by prioritising the health of your employees, you're also investing in the health of your business.

RECAP AND ACTION ITEMS

Alright, now that we've delved deeply into the essentials of risk management within the warehousing sector, it's paramount to take these insights and translate them into actionable strategies that you can implement in your operations. Managing warehouse risks, preparing for emergencies, and monitoring health are not just regulatory requirements but pivotal elements that can define the success and safety of your logistics business.

First up, revisit the common warehouse hazards identified and cross-check these with your current workplace. It's crucial that you periodically assess your storage facilities for any new risks that might have emerged. Remember, safety is not a one-time audit but a continuous process of improvement. Initiate quarterly safety reviews and encourage your team to report any potential hazards they notice.

Moving on to safe storage practices and equipment safety, consider implementing regular training sessions for your team. This ensures everyone is updated on the best practices and understands how to use equipment safely. These sessions could be a mix of in-person and digital training modules, depending on what fits best with your operational schedule.

Now, let's talk about emergency preparedness. Having a solid emergency plan isn't just about compliance; it's about readiness that can save lives and resources. If you haven't already, develop or refine your emergency response plan. Conduct drills regularly so that your team isn't just aware of the procedures but is also well-practiced in executing them under pressure.

For fire safety management, ensure that your equipment, alarms, and fire suppression systems are in top shape. Regular checks and maintenance can be the difference between a minor incident and a major catastrophe.

Regarding accident response strategies, streamline your processes for reporting and responding to incidents. Quick and efficient response not only minimises harm but also helps in faster recovery and resumption of operations.

Finally, in the area of health surveillance and monitoring, initiate a program if you haven't got one yet. Regular health checks, exposure monitoring, and occupational illness prevention plans are essential. These not only help in ensuring compliance with health and safety regulations but also in encouraging a workplace environment that prioritises employee well-being.

Remember, the steps you take today to improve risk management in your warehousing operations can significantly impact your organisation's future resilience and efficiency. Consider these strategies as investments into the long-term success and safety of your business. Start implementing these actions and set the standard for excellence in logistics and warehousing.

3

Optimising Safety in Logistics Operations

"Safety does not happen by accident." - Unknown

Transportation Safety

In the high-stakes world of logistics and warehousing, ensuring the safety of transportation operations isn't just about compliance—it's a cornerstone of operational excellence. As you navigate the complexities of this dynamic field, focusing on vehicle maintenance, driver safety programs, and safe loading and unloading procedures will not only mitigate risks but also enhance efficiency and protect your bottom line. Let's dive into these critical components.

Vehicle Maintenance

First off, vehicle maintenance is not where you want to cut corners. Regular and thorough maintenance checks are essential to keep your fleet running smoothly and safely. This approach goes beyond mere compliance with safety regulations—it's about creating a proactive culture that prioritises well-being and efficiency.

Start by establishing a rigorous maintenance schedule that aligns with the manufacturer's recommendations and legal requirements. Each vehicle in your fleet should have a detailed service log, updated regularly, to track its maintenance history. This log should be digital whenever possible to facilitate real-time updates and easy access.

Investing in predictive maintenance technologies can also offer you a significant advantage. These systems use data analytics and machine learning to predict when a vehicle might need maintenance before it becomes apparent. This can help you avoid the downtime associated with unexpected breakdowns and the potential safety hazards they create.

Moreover, ensure that your maintenance team is well-trained and equipped. They should not only understand the specifics of each vehicle but also be adept at spotting early signs of wear and tear that could escalate into larger issues. Regular training sessions and workshops can keep them up-to-date with the latest technological advancements and repair techniques.

Driver Safety Programs

Moving on to driver safety programs, remember, your drivers are as crucial as your fleet. They need to be competent, alert, and aware of safety practices to navigate the complexities of modern roads safely.

Develop a comprehensive driver training program that covers not only the basics of safe driving but also advanced defensive driving techniques. Include modules on fatigue management, hazard recognition, and emergency response. It's also beneficial to incorporate simulation training to help drivers prepare for a variety of scenarios they might encounter on the road.

Another key element is continuous assessment. Regularly evaluate your drivers through practical driving tests and knowledge assessments to ensure they remain sharp and aware of the best practices in vehicle safety.

Encourage a culture of safety among your drivers by making it a core part of your organisation's values. Recognition programs for safe driving records and open forums for drivers to share their experiences and suggestions can encourage this culture.

Safe Loading and Unloading Procedures

Finally, let's tackle safe loading and unloading procedures—areas ripe for accidents if not managed properly. The loading dock can be a hub of activity where even small oversights may lead to significant injuries or damage.

Start by ensuring that your loading docks are designed and maintained with safety in mind. This includes clear signage, proper lighting, and ensuring that surfaces are even and free from hazards. Dock levellers should be regularly inspected and maintained to facilitate safe transfers between the warehouse and transport vehicles.

Training is pivotal here as well. Staff involved in loading and unloading should be trained in the correct procedures to prevent falls, strains, and equipment mishaps. They should be equipped with the proper personal protective equipment (PPE) and understand how to use it correctly.

Implement strict procedures for securing loads. Incorrectly secured cargo can shift during transport, posing serious risks to safety. Use of restraint methods like straps, chains, and load bars should be standard practice, with regular inspections to ensure they are fit for purpose.

Automation and mechanical aids can significantly enhance safety in loading operations. Investment in equipment such as pallet jacks, forklifts, and automated conveyor systems can reduce manual handling injuries and improve the efficiency of loading operations. Ensure that all operators are fully trained and certified to use this equipment, and that it's regularly maintained.

By focusing on these three key areas—vehicle maintenance, driver safety programs, and safe loading and unloading procedures—you can significantly uplift the safety standards of your transportation operations. Each element not only contributes to reducing risks but also enhances the overall efficiency and reputation of your logistics and warehousing operations. As you continue to refine these practices, remember that safety is an ongoing journey, requiring persistent dedication and adaptability to new challenges and technologies.

Handling Goods Safely

When it comes to logistics and warehousing operations, the way you handle goods not only impacts the efficiency of your operations but also the safety of your team. Let's deep dive into the best practices that can bolster safety while ensuring the smooth flow of operations.

Manual Handling Techniques

It's no secret that the backbone of warehouse operations often relies on the literal backs of your workforce. Manual handling, if not done correctly, can lead to a significant number of work-related injuries. These are not only detrimental to the health of your employees but can also lead to increased absenteeism, reduced productivity, and potentially hefty compensation claims.

First and foremost, education is key. Ensuring that your team understands the mechanics of their bodies and the principles of safe lifting can drastically reduce the risk of injuries. Simple techniques such as keeping the load close to the waist, maintaining a stable and straight back, bending at the knees (not the back), and avoiding twisting movements while lifting should be ingrained practices.

Moreover, consider the layout of your warehouse. Are items stored at a sensible height? Are heavier objects placed in a way that minimises the need for awkward lifting? Small adjustments in the organisation of your space can lead to big reductions in risk.

Workshops and regular refresher courses on manual handling can also be invaluable. Remember, people are your most precious commodity, and investing in their well-being is directly investing in the success and safety of your operations.

Mechanical Aids

While manual handling skills are crucial, reducing the need for manual handling altogether through mechanical aids can be even more effective. Equipment such as forklifts, pallet jacks, conveyor belts, and even automated robotic solutions can take much of the physical strain away from your team.

Investing in the right tools for the job not only boosts safety but also efficiency. For instance, using a forklift for moving heavy pallets is exponentially safer and quicker than having team members move them manually. However, it's vital to ensure that each piece of equipment is suitable for the specific tasks and the environment in which it's used.

Training becomes a non-negotiable aspect when it comes to operating mechanical aids. It's not just about knowing how to use the equipment but understanding the safety protocols associated with each. Regular maintenance checks are also essential to ensure that these aids remain safe to use. A broken conveyor belt or a malfunctioning forklift is not just a productivity killer but a major safety hazard.

Training for Handling Equipment

The importance of training cannot be overstressed. Whether it's manual handling techniques or the operation of mechanical aids, competent training is the bedrock of safe handling practices. This is not a one-time event but an ongoing process. As technologies evolve and new equipment is introduced, your training programmes should adapt and evolve too.

It's advisable to have a structured training programme in place that includes both initial and periodic refresher training. Utilising experienced, knowledgeable trainers who can engage with staff and adapt their teaching methods to different learning styles can greatly enhance the effectiveness of your training.

Moreover, don't just restrict your training to the 'how' but also focus on the 'why'. Helping your team understand the reasons behind safety procedures increases their commitment to following these guidelines. It also empowers them to identify potential risks and take proactive steps to mitigate them.

Incorporating feedback mechanisms where employees can share their insights and feedback about the handling processes and training can also lead you to uncover potential areas for improvement. After all, those on the ground often have the clearest view of the risks and inefficiencies.

In conclusion, handling goods safely in your logistics and warehousing operations is a multifaceted endeavour that hinges on proper techniques, the right tools, and robust training programmes. By focusing on these areas, you ensure not just compliance with safety standards but also create a work environment that prioritises the well-being of your employees. The knock-on effect is a more efficient, productive, and ultimately more profitable operation. Remember, a safer warehouse is your step towards a more successful business.

Environmental Considerations

Navigating the complexities of environmental management in logistics can often feel like trying to solve a Rubik's Cube in the dark. However, with the right strategies in place, you can not only enhance your company's sustainability but also its overall efficiency and compliance with ever-tightening regulations. Let's dive into three critical areas: Waste Management, Controlling Emissions, and Spill Response.

Waste Management

In the logistics and warehousing sector, waste management is not just about disposing of materials responsibly; it's about rethinking the entire lifecycle of the resources you use. Start by assessing your current waste streams. What are you throwing away? More importantly, why are you throwing it away? By understanding the 'what' and 'why', you can begin to find ways to reduce, reuse, and recycle materials more effectively.

Consider implementing a waste audit to get a clearer picture. This involves examining the waste produced at different points in your operations to identify the primary sources of waste and opportunities for minimisation. The results can often be eye-opening and can direct you towards making changes that not only reduce environmental impact but also cut costs.

Once you've identified key waste sources, look at your procurement practices. Can you switch to suppliers who use minimal packaging or who take back packaging for reuse? Such changes, while seemingly small, can significantly reduce the volume of waste your operations generate.

Furthermore, engaging your team is crucial. Training staff on new waste management protocols and the reasons behind them can encourage a culture of sustainability. Remember, every employee who understands the value of recycling and waste reduction becomes a champion of sustainability in your operations.

Controlling Emissions

Emissions in logistics primarily stem from transportation and the machinery used in warehouses. Tackling this starts with optimising your transport routes. Advanced route planning software can reduce unnecessary travel, thereby cutting down on fuel consumption and emissions. Also, consider the potential of electric and hybrid vehicles in your fleet. With the UK's focus on reducing carbon footprints, transitioning to cleaner technologies is not just an environmental decision but a strategic business move.

In your warehouses, machinery like forklifts can produce significant emissions. Switching to electric models offers an immediate reduction in carbon emissions and often results in lower long-term operational costs due to decreased maintenance and fuel expenses. Additionally, explore opportunities for using renewable energy sources such as solar panels on warehouse roofs. This not only reduces reliance on fossil fuels but can also provide financial benefits through government incentives and reduced energy bills.

It's also worth exploring the latest in environmental technology innovations. For example, telematics can be used to monitor vehicle emissions in real-time, allowing for immediate adjustments and long-term strategy enhancements. This type of technology not only helps in controlling emissions but can also be a critical tool in reporting for compliance and sustainability goals.

Spill Response

Despite best efforts, spills can occur, and how you respond to them can significantly influence their environmental impact. Having a robust spill response plan is essential. This plan should include immediate containment measures, strategies for notifying environmental agencies (if required), and detailed processes for cleanup and waste disposal.

Start by ensuring that all employees are trained in basic spill response techniques. This includes understanding the types of materials that are likely to spill and the specific hazards associated with each. They should know how to use spill kits effectively and understand the importance of acting quickly to prevent environmental contamination.

Next, consider the placement of spill kits throughout your facilities. They should be easily accessible and close to high-risk areas. Regular checks are crucial to ensure that these kits are fully stocked and that all components are in good working order.

For larger or more hazardous spills, professional environmental services may be necessary to ensure proper handling and disposal. Establish relationships with trusted environmental service providers before you need them. This proactive approach can make all the difference in effectively managing a spill.

Implementing these strategies requires an upfront investment of time and resources, but the payoff comes in the form of reduced environmental impact, enhanced compliance with regulations, and often, significant cost savings. As a senior manager or director, leading the charge in these initiatives not only positions your company as a responsible corporate citizen but also sets you apart as a visionary leader in the logistics and warehousing industry.

By integrating comprehensive waste management practices, advanced emission control technologies, and effective spill response plans, you create a resilient framework that supports sustainable operations. This not only aligns with environmental goals but also enhances operational efficiency and readiness for future regulatory changes. Remember, the goal is not just to respond to environmental challenges but to anticipate and strategically manage them for long-term sustainability and success.

RECAP AND ACTION ITEMS

Optimising safety in logistics operations isn't just about ticking off boxes on compliance checklists—it's about cultivating an environment where safety is woven into the very fabric of your operations. From the meticulous maintenance of your vehicles to the precision and care in manual and mechanical handling of goods, each element plays a crucial role in safeguarding your workforce and boosting overall productivity.

Firstly, let's reflect on the essential practices of vehicle maintenance. Ensuring that each vehicle in your fleet is operating at peak condition is not just a regulatory requirement—it's a fundamental component of your operational integrity. Take proactive steps by scheduling regular check-ups and embracing technology that aids in regular diagnostics. Implementing a robust maintenance schedule isn't just about preventing breakdowns; it's an investment in the reliability and safety of your entire operation.

Moving on to driver safety programs and safe loading and unloading procedures, consider these as your frontline defence against workplace accidents. Cultivating a culture where safety training is not just a one-off but a continuous engagement can dramatically reduce risks. Explore interactive and regular training sessions that focus on real-world scenarios that your drivers and loading staff might face.

In handling goods safely, your approach should balance manual techniques with mechanical aids. It's crucial to have your staff trained not only in proper manual handling techniques but also in the effective use of mechanical aids. This dual approach minimises the risk of injury and enhances efficiency. Ensure that your training programs are updated regularly to keep pace with new equipment and techniques.

Lastly, environmental considerations such as waste management, controlling emissions, and spill response are not only about compliance with environmental regulations but also about your company's role in encouraging a sustainable future. Implement systems that ensure quick and effective responses to spills, and strategies that reduce emissions and efficiently manage waste.

Now, for the action steps:1. Conduct an audit of your current safety practices and identify areas for immediate improvement

2. Set up a quarterly review of your vehicle maintenance logs and driver safety records

3. Invest in training programs that are both engaging and comprehensive, covering everything from manual handling to emergency response

4. Explore the latest innovations in mechanical aids and evaluate their potential integration into your operations

5. Develop a clear, actionable environmental policy if you haven't already, and ensure it's communicated effectively to all levels of your staff.

By taking these steps, you're not just complying with regulations—you're setting a standard in your industry and ensuring that safety is at the heart of your logistics operations.

4

Cultivating A Safety Culture

"Culture eats strategy for breakfast, but safety sustains it for a lifetime." - Peter Drucker

Leadership in Safety

Safety in the logistics and warehousing sector isn't just a regulatory requirement; it's a cornerstone of effective operational leadership. As a senior manager or director, your approach to safety sets the tone for your entire organisation. In this section, we will explore how you, as a leader, can enhance safety protocols not just by enforcing them, but by embodying them.

Role of Senior Management

As a leader in logistics and warehousing, your primary role in safety management extends beyond mere compliance; it involves cultivating a culture where safety is valued as paramount. The decisions you make, the priorities you set, and the behaviours you model all influence how safety is perceived and practised within your organisation.

Firstly, it's crucial to integrate safety into your strategic objectives. This integration shows your workforce that you value safety as much as productivity and efficiency. For instance, when setting annual goals, include specific safety targets such as reducing incident rates or improving near-miss reporting. These targets should be SMART: Specific, Measurable, Achievable, Relevant, and Time-bound.

Secondly, ensure that your leadership team is aligned with your safety vision. This alignment means regularly discussing safety in management meetings and holding leaders accountable for safety outcomes in their departments. When every member of your senior management team communicates the same safety messages, it reinforces their importance, leading to a more cohesive and safety-focused organisational culture.

Moreover, investing in the right tools and technologies plays a crucial role. Whether it's advanced warehouse management systems (WMS) that ensure safe and efficient operations or ergonomic tools that reduce physical strain on your employees, showing that you're willing to invest in safety enhances its value within the company.

Setting Safety Goals

Setting safety goals is not just about reducing the number of accidents; it's about creating an environment where safety is an integral part of the operational process. To do this effectively, involve your team in the goal-setting process. This inclusion not only increases buy-in but also leverages their on-the-ground experience to identify achievable targets.

When setting these goals, consider both lagging and leading indicators. Lagging indicators, such as accident rates, are helpful but they only tell part of the story. Leading indicators — like safety training attendance, safety audits, or proactive maintenance checks — can provide insights into your safety culture's health before accidents occur.

One effective strategy is to set tiered goals. Start with broad objectives at the corporate level, then distil these into more specific targets for individual departments or teams. For example, if a general goal is to reduce workplace accidents by 20% year-on-year, a specific target for the warehouse team could be to implement a new spill management training program by the end of Q2.

Remember, the key to successful goal setting in safety is visibility and consistency. Regularly review these goals in your communications and ensure they are prominently displayed around the workplace. Regular updates on progress towards these goals can also serve as a motivational tool and a reminder of their importance.

Leading by Example

The adage "actions speak louder than words" holds particularly true in safety leadership. You can set all the safety goals you want, but if you don't adhere to them yourself, they won't resonate with your team. Leading by example means following safety protocols diligently, even when it might be quicker or easier to skip steps.

When you consistently wear the required personal protective equipment (PPE), follow proper procedures, and actively participate in safety training sessions, you not only reinforce their importance but also demonstrate your commitment to your team's well-being. It's also effective to be involved in safety briefings and not just leave these to your safety officers. Your presence at these briefings can significantly boost their weight.

Moreover, your reaction to safety incidents matters immensely. Instead of placing blame, focus on what can be learned from the incident. This approach encourages an open environment where employees feel safe to report risks or mistakes, knowing that the focus will be on solutions and prevention rather than punishment.

In conclusion, as a leader in logistics and warehousing, your role in encouraging a safety-centric culture is pivotal. By integrating safety into your strategic planning, setting clear and collaborative safety goals, and leading by example, you not only ensure compliance but also drive operational excellence. Remember, a safe warehouse is an efficient warehouse.

Employee Engagement

Engaging employees in safety practices is not just about compliance or following rules. It's about creating an environment where safety is part of the culture and everyone feels responsible for it. This segment explores effective ways to boost employee engagement through incentives, communication strategies, and feedback loops.

Incentives for Safe Behaviour

Let's talk incentives. Everyone likes a pat on the back, right? Especially when it's for keeping themselves and their colleagues safe. Incentivising safe behaviour isn't about handing out bonuses for every accident-free day—although that can be part of it. It's about creating a reward system that recognises and reinforces the value of safety in every task.

Firstly, consider introducing a points system where employees earn points for daily or weekly safe practices. These can be simple things like wearing safety gear, completing safety checks, or innovatively improving workplace safety. Points could then be exchanged for rewards such as gift cards, extra holiday time, or even public recognition in front of peers.

Another angle is peer-to-peer recognition programmes. Enable your team to nominate colleagues for safety awards. This not only boosts the morale of the nominated employee but also encourages others to emulate safe behaviours. It encourages a sense of teamwork and accountability, which are crucial ingredients for a sustainable safety culture.

Remember, the key here is consistency and fairness in how rewards are given. Rewards need to be attainable and desirable. If they feel unachievable or insignificant, they won't motivate your team. Keep the lines of communication open to understand what kinds of incentives will most resonate with your employees.

Communication Strategies

Communication is the glue that holds your safety culture together. Without it, even the most well-thought-out plans can falter. For senior managers and directors, effective communication means more than sending out monthly safety newsletters or the occasional bulletin.

Start with regular safety meetings that don't just dictate policies but allow for two-way dialogues. These meetings should be safe spaces where employees can express concerns and contribute ideas without fear of repercussions. It's about encouraging an open-door policy where safety discussions are as normal as talking about the weekend game.

Technology can also play a pivotal role here. Consider using mobile apps or an intranet site dedicated to safety in the workplace. These platforms can host virtual meetings, real-time safety updates, and educational resources. They are also excellent for reaching diverse teams, particularly useful if your operations span multiple sites or include remote workers.

But let's not forget the power of informal communications. Sometimes, a casual chat on the warehouse floor about safety can be more effective than any formal meeting. It shows that you, as a leader, are approachable and genuinely concerned about safety, which can significantly influence the workplace atmosphere.

Feedback and Improvement Loops

Lastly, let's nail down the importance of feedback and improvement loops. This is where you close the gap between strategy and real-world application. You've set the safety goals, communicated them, and incentivised safe practices. Now, how do you ensure these are working effectively?

Implement regular feedback mechanisms. Surveys, suggestion boxes, and follow-up meetings post-incident are excellent tools for gathering insights. Make it easy and anonymous, if possible, to encourage honest feedback. The data collected from these sources is gold dust for identifying areas where safety measures might be falling short or where new risks have emerged.

Once feedback is collected, loop it back into your safety programmes. This could mean adjusting training procedures, tweaking incentive schemes, or even overhauling certain safety protocols. Regular audits and reviews play a crucial role here, ensuring that no part of your safety strategy becomes outdated or ineffective.

Moreover, use this feedback to celebrate successes. If a particular strategy has led to a noticeable improvement in safety, share this with the team. Highlight how their efforts have made a difference, reinforcing the value of everyone's contribution to a safer workplace.

In essence, engaging your employees in safety isn't a one-off project. It's a continuous pursuit that requires creativity, commitment, and genuine concern for the wellbeing of your people. By focusing on meaningful incentives, robust communication, and dynamic feedback loops, you can embed safety into the fabric of your daily operations, ensuring it becomes more than just a compliance requirement—it becomes a way of life at your warehouse.

Continuous Improvement

When it comes to safety culture in logistics and warehousing, resting on your laurels isn't an option. Continuous improvement is the name of the game, ensuring that safety processes not only meet current standards but are also geared up for future challenges. Let's delve into three pivotal areas: Safety Audits, Benchmarking, and Utilising Safety Metrics, each playing a crucial role in keeping your operations both safe and compliant.

Safety Audits

Think of safety audits not as a necessary evil, but as a powerful tool in your arsenal to promote and maintain a culture of safety. Regular audits provide a structured opportunity to identify potential hazards before they lead to incidents. More than just ticking boxes, these audits are about gaining insights and finding real opportunities for improvement.

Start by establishing a schedule that doesn't just comply with the minimum legal requirements but goes beyond to reflect the unique dynamics of your operations. Frequency is key, and so is depth. Each audit should be thorough enough to cover all areas of your warehouse or logistical operations, leaving no stone unturned.

The methodology you adopt for conducting these audits can significantly influence their effectiveness. Incorporate both qualitative and quantitative assessment techniques. Use checklists for consistency but encourage auditors to also make narrative notes when they spot potential issues or good practices that aren't covered by standard checklist items.

Training for auditors should be robust. They need to understand not just what they're checking for but why. Each auditor should be able to discern the implications of the audit findings in the broader context of operational safety and efficiency.

Lastly, ensure that the findings from each audit are documented meticulously and reviewed at a senior level. This review should culminate in actionable steps that are assigned and tracked to completion. It's this cycle of review and improvement that transforms standard auditing into a potent tool for enhancing safety culture.

Benchmarking

Benchmarking is your window to the industry's best practices and a reality check for how your safety measures stack up against peers. This process involves looking outward to understand where you are positioned in the industry and inward to identify areas for improvement.

Begin by selecting metrics that matter. These could range from incident rates to employee safety training completion percentages. Choose benchmarks that are ambitious yet achievable, ensuring they push your organisation towards excellence without setting you up for failure.

Engaging with industry groups and forums can be invaluable here. These platforms allow you to exchange data and insights with other firms, offering a broader perspective on what's working elsewhere. However, remember that the goal of benchmarking is not to replicate but to adapt. What works for one may not work for another; the key is to learn, adapt, and implement in a way that aligns with your specific operational needs and corporate culture.

Implementing changes based on benchmarking insights should be approached with a structured change management process. This ensures that any adjustments to operations are made systematically and with buy-in from all levels of the organisation, particularly from those who are on the ground and most affected by these changes.

Utilising Safety Metrics

Metrics are your indicators of how well your safety initiatives are performing. They provide the quantitative data needed to support qualitative assessments and are essential for informed decision-making.

First, identify which metrics will provide you with a clear picture of your safety landscape. Commonly tracked metrics in logistics and warehousing include accident frequency rates, near-miss cases, safety training completion rates, and compliance scores. However, the trick isn't just in choosing them but in how you use them to drive safety improvements.

Utilising these metrics effectively requires setting up a dashboard that senior management can review regularly. This dashboard should highlight trends, pinpoint areas of concern, and track improvements over time. It should be capable of drilling down into data when needed to uncover root causes of safety issues.

Moreover, integrating real-time data collection can significantly enhance the utility of your safety metrics. With advancements in technology, including IoT devices and AI, you can monitor operational parameters continuously and receive alerts when certain thresholds are breached, allowing for swift corrective actions.

Finally, the communication of these metrics and their implications must be clear and widespread across the organisation. Every team member should understand what the metrics indicate, why they matter, and how their actions contribute to the bigger picture. This encourages a shared responsibility towards safety, reinforcing its importance at every level of your operations.

Continuous improvement in safety isn't just about reducing risks or complying with laws; it's a fundamental component of operational excellence. By focusing on rigorous safety audits, insightful benchmarking, and strategic use of safety metrics, you ensure that your safety culture is not static but a dynamic, integral part of your organisation's success. Remember, in the fast-evolving world of logistics and warehousing, staying still is not an option. Keep pushing the boundaries, and let safety be the compass that guides every decision you make.

RECAP AND ACTION ITEMS

Cultivating a safety culture within your logistics and warehousing operations isn't just about compliance; it's a strategic move that can significantly enhance productivity, employee morale, and your company's reputation. You've explored the pivotal role of senior management in establishing and nurturing this culture, setting clear and achievable safety goals, and the importance of leading by example.

To translate these insights into action, start by revisiting your current safety policies. Are they clear, comprehensive, and truly reflective of the safety-first ethos you aspire to? If not, it's time for an overhaul. Engage with your leadership team to ensure that everyone is aligned and committed to these goals. Remember, the tone you set at the top cascades down through all levels of your organisation.

Next, focus on employee engagement. Begin by reviewing your current incentives for safe behaviour. Are they effective? Do they motivate your team in a meaningful way? Consider innovative communication strategies that encourage a two-way dialogue, such as regular safety forums or digital platforms where employees can voice concerns and suggestions. Importantly, establish robust feedback and improvement loops. Action the feedback received; this demonstrates to your team that their input is valued and acted upon, which can significantly boost morale and adherence to safety protocols.

Lastly, embed continuous improvement into your safety practices. Regular safety audits are crucial, but they must be complemented by benchmarking against industry standards and utilising safety metrics to track progress. These steps will help you identify areas for improvement and gauge the effectiveness of your safety initiatives.

Your action steps? Conduct a safety policy review meeting within the next two weeks. Schedule a session to brainstorm new incentives for safe behaviour. Implement a new communication strategy and set up the first feedback loop by the end of the quarter. Finally, plan your next safety audit, set benchmarking parameters, and establish a system for regular review of safety metrics.

By systematically applying these strategies, you can ensure that safety becomes more than just a compliance requirement—it becomes a cornerstone of your operational excellence and leadership in the logistics and warehousing sector.

5

Technological Innovations Enhancing Safety

"Technology is not just an enabler, but a guardian of safety, forging a path where innovation meets protection." – Elon Musk

Digital Solutions for Risk Management

In the fast-paced world of logistics and warehousing, staying ahead of risks not only ensures operational efficiency but also guards the safety of your staff and compliance with stringent regulations. Embracing digital solutions is not just a forward-thinking move; it's becoming a fundamental necessity. Let's explore how technology is reshaping risk management in your industry, from software that streamlines risk assessments to AI that keeps a vigilant eye on compliance.

Use of Software for Risk Assessments

Risk assessments are the backbone of safety and compliance in logistics and warehousing. Traditionally, these assessments were carried out manually, a process fraught with the potential for human error and often incredibly time-consuming. Enter risk assessment software, a game-changer for your operations.

This software automates and simplifies the identification of potential hazards in your warehouse or logistics chain. By integrating this technology, you can swiftly analyse various risk factors associated with equipment, operations, and environmental conditions. The software typically employs a database of known hazards which can be updated with new information, ensuring that the risk assessments are up-to-date and relevant.

Moreover, this digital approach allows for dynamic risk assessments. For instance, if a new piece of equipment is introduced or a workflow is altered, the software can immediately evaluate the new risks associated with these changes. This real-time capability ensures that you are always a step ahead, maintaining a safe working environment.

The beauty of using such software lies in its ability to collate and organise data into actionable insights. You can generate reports that not only help in complying with health and safety legislation but also in making informed decisions that enhance operational efficiency. By reducing the administrative burden, your teams can focus more on core operations, driving productivity.

Mobile Apps for Safety Training

Training is crucial in ensuring that every member of your team understands the potential hazards and knows how to handle them safely. Mobile apps are revolutionising how training is delivered in the logistics and warehousing sector. These apps provide interactive and user-friendly platforms through which employees can access training materials anytime and anywhere, breaking the constraints of traditional classroom settings.

Imagine an app that offers video tutorials, interactive simulations, and quizzes tailored to the specific needs of your operations. Such tools not only make learning more engaging but also improve the retention of safety protocols.

Employees can revisit the training materials as often as needed, reinforcing safe practices.

Additionally, these apps can be updated swiftly to reflect any changes in safety regulations or operational procedures. This flexibility ensures that your training programme is always in sync with current standards without incurring significant downtime or additional costs.

The use of mobile apps for safety training also facilitates better tracking and management of training outcomes. You can monitor who has completed the training, assess their understanding through quizzes, and even receive feedback to continuously improve the training content.

AI in Monitoring Compliance

Compliance with health and safety regulations is non-negotiable. Artificial Intelligence (AI) is proving to be an indispensable ally in monitoring and ensuring compliance across multiple facets of logistics and warehousing operations.

AI-powered systems can continuously analyse data from various sources within your operations, such as CCTV footage, sensor data from machinery, and logs from digital training modules. By leveraging machine learning algorithms, these systems can identify patterns and predict potential compliance issues before they become actual problems.

For example, an AI system could analyse video feeds to ensure that all employees are wearing the necessary safety gear at all times within the warehouse. It could also highlight areas where there is frequent non-compliance, allowing you to focus your safety training more effectively.

Moreover, AI can handle the vast amounts of documentation associated with compliance. From managing safety records to ensuring that all required reports are filed on time, AI can automate these processes, reducing the risk of human error and freeing up your team to focus on more strategic tasks.

By integrating AI into your compliance monitoring efforts, you can maintain a high level of safety standards while also adhering to legal requirements. This proactive approach not only helps in avoiding costly penalties but also enhances the overall safety culture within your organisation.

As you can see, digital solutions are transforming the landscape of risk management in logistics and warehousing. By adopting these technologies, you are not only enhancing safety and compliance but also positioning your operations to thrive in an increasingly competitive market. Embrace these innovations and lead your team with confidence into a safer, more efficient future.

The Role of Automation

Automation in the logistics and warehousing sector isn't just about replacing manual tasks with robots; it's about revolutionising the safety standards and efficiency of operations. As a senior manager or director, understanding these technological shifts is crucial not just for operational excellence but also for the safety and well-being of your workforce.

Automated Storage and Retrieval Systems (ASRS)

Imagine a system so finely tuned that it can manage and retrieve goods with minimal human intervention, operating in a high-density setup that maximises space and minimises risk. That's the beauty of Automated Storage and Retrieval Systems. These systems are designed to handle loads of all sizes and types, from small parts to large pallets, ensuring that storage is not only space-efficient but also less prone to accidents that can occur with manual handling.

The implementation of ASRS dramatically reduces the need for staff to engage in potentially hazardous tasks, such as climbing on racking to retrieve items or operating heavy lifting equipment. Instead, goods are moved automatically to a retrieval area, significantly lowering the risk of workplace injuries. For you, this means a safer environment and a more streamlined operation, where the risk of human error is markedly reduced and efficiency is heightened.

But the benefits don't stop at safety and space optimisation. ASRS can lead to a decrease in damaged goods. Automated systems are precise and can be adjusted to handle products with care, mitigating the risk of manual handling errors. Additionally, these systems can operate in environments that are less hospitable to humans, such as cold storage, further ensuring worker safety by reducing exposure to harsh conditions.

Robotics in Logistics

The integration of robotics in logistics goes beyond automated machinery moving stock around a warehouse. Today's robots can collaborate with humans, working alongside your team to enhance their capabilities rather than replace them.

Take collaborative robots, or cobots, which are designed to interact with humans in a shared space or to work independently alongside human workers. These cobots are equipped with sensors and AI capabilities that enable them to understand and adapt to their environment, making them safe for use around humans. They can perform repetitive, strenuous tasks, reducing human fatigue and the associated risk of injuries.

Moreover, robotics in logistics isn't limited to just lifting and moving. Robots can also be equipped with advanced vision systems and AI-driven decision-making capabilities, allowing them to pick, sort, and pack goods with high precision and speed. This not only boosts efficiency but also minimises the chances of accidents and errors that can occur in manual processes.

Investing in robotics may seem like a hefty upfront cost, but the long-term savings and safety improvements can be substantial. Reduced injury-related costs, higher throughput, and lower human resource expenditure due to task automation are just a few financial upsides to this technological investment.

Impact on Worker Safety

While discussing automation, it's imperative to focus on its impact on worker safety, which is a significant concern in the logistics and warehousing sector. The introduction of automated systems and robotics has been shown to decrease the number of accidents and injuries dramatically.

Automated systems can be programmed to follow strict safety protocols and can operate in controlled environments designed to minimise human error and safety hazards. For instance, ASRS and robotics eliminate the need for workers to engage in high-risk activities such as working at height or manual lifting and carrying heavy items.

Furthermore, these systems can also contribute to a healthier workplace by undertaking tasks in environments that are not conducive to human health, such as extreme temperatures or poor air quality areas. By automating these processes, you're not only safeguarding your employees' physical health but also ensuring compliance with health and safety regulations, which is paramount in maintaining operational licenses and avoiding legal repercussions.

However, it's crucial to continue investing in safety training and maintenance. Automation systems require regular checks and updates to ensure they operate efficiently and safely. Moreover, as the workplace becomes more intertwined with technology, the nature of safety training also needs to evolve. Training programmes should include modules on interacting safely with automated systems and understanding the basics of robotic operations, ensuring that your team is equipped not just to coexist with these technologies but to thrive alongside them.

In embracing automation, you're not just investing in technology; you're investing in a safer, more efficient future for your logistics and warehousing operations. The transition may require substantial change management and capital investment, but the potential returns in enhanced safety, efficiency, and compliance are immense. As you continue to navigate the complexities of the logistics and warehousing industry, consider how automation can not only meet but exceed your safety and operational goals.

Wearable Safety Technology

In the fast-paced world of logistics and warehousing, the adoption of wearable safety technology is not just a trend but a game-changer in enhancing worker safety and operational efficiency. As you navigate the complexities of managing large-scale operations, understanding the nuances of these technologies can significantly impact your strategy for safety and compliance.

Smart Helmets

One of the standout innovations in wearable safety technology is the smart helmet. Picture this: your warehouse workers equipped with helmets that not only protect their heads but also feed them vital information through a heads-up display. Smart helmets integrate augmented reality (AR) to overlay digital information onto the physical environment. This can include data about inventory levels, safety hazards, and operational instructions, all visible without the need to look away from their tasks.

The benefits of smart helmets extend beyond just data provision. They can also enhance safety through features like thermal imaging and environmental monitoring sensors. These sensors can detect hazardous conditions such as extreme temperatures or the presence of toxic gases, alerting the wearer to potential danger before it becomes a threat. For you, this means a proactive approach to managing workplace safety, reducing the risk of accidents and their associated costs.

Moreover, smart helmets can be integrated with other systems. For instance, linking them to your incident management software allows for immediate reporting and response to any safety issues. This integration not only speeds up your reaction times but also facilitates a more detailed analysis of incidents, helping you refine your safety protocols continuously.

Exoskeletons for Lifting

Exoskeletons are another transformative technology in the realm of wearable safety devices. These mechanical suits support your workers physically, particularly when lifting and moving heavy items. By augmenting human strength, exoskeletons reduce the strain on the body, thereby minimising the risk of musculoskeletal injuries which are all too common in the warehousing sector.

The adoption of exoskeletons can be a strategic move for boosting not only safety but also productivity. Workers equipped with these devices can handle heavier loads and work for longer periods without fatigue. This capability makes them invaluable during peak operational times when demand surges and the pace of work intensifies.

From a management perspective, exoskeletons represent a significant investment in worker health and operational capacity. They send a clear message that you prioritise worker wellbeing, which can enhance staff morale and loyalty—a crucial factor in industries facing skill shortages and high turnover rates.

Real-time Health Monitoring Devices

Finally, let's talk about real-time health monitoring devices. These wearables, which can range from smartwatches to specialised garments, monitor vital signs and other health metrics such as heart rate, body temperature, and stress levels. The ability to track this physiological data in real time presents a unique opportunity for you to safeguard your workforce proactively.

Imagine being able to receive alerts if a worker's heart rate spikes or body temperature deviates from normal levels, indicating stress or illness. This capability allows you to take immediate action, perhaps by pulling them off a task or providing a break, thereby preventing potential accidents or health issues.

Moreover, the data collected from these devices can be analysed to identify patterns or trends that may indicate underlying issues within your operations. Perhaps certain tasks are consistently causing stress or fatigue, suggesting a need for process adjustments or further training. By addressing these issues, you can improve worker satisfaction and efficiency, reducing turnover and boosting overall productivity.

Incorporating real-time health monitoring into your operations also demonstrates a commitment to an advanced level of duty of care. It reassures your team that their health and safety are being watched over meticulously, encouraging a culture of trust and safety.

In conclusion, as you continue to steer your logistics and warehousing operations through the challenges and opportunities of the 21st century, wearable safety technology offers powerful tools for enhancing worker safety, compliance, and efficiency. Whether through smart helmets, exoskeletons, or health monitoring devices, these innovations are set to revolutionise the way you manage and protect your most valuable asset—your people. Embracing these technologies not only positions you as a forward-thinking leader but also solidifies your commitment to a safer, more productive workplace.

RECAP AND ACTION ITEMS

You've journeyed through an array of cutting-edge technologies that have the power to transform how safety is managed in the logistics and warehousing sectors. From digital tools for risk assessments, mobile apps for safety training, to AI-driven compliance monitoring, these innovations offer a new dimension in proactive safety management. Furthermore, automation technologies like Automated Storage and Retrieval Systems and robotics are not just reshaping operations but are also setting new standards in worker safety. Wearable technologies, including smart helmets, exoskeletons, and real-time health monitoring devices, are pioneering personal safety and ergonomics.

Now, let's convert insight into action.

1. Evaluate Your Current Technology: Start by reviewing the current technological tools your organisation utilises. Identify gaps where emerging technologies could enhance safety and compliance. Are there areas in your risk management that could benefit from more accurate and timely data provided by AI and software solutions?

2. Pilot Innovative Solutions: Select a technology you are not currently using, such as exoskeletons for lifting or AI in compliance monitoring. Implement a pilot project to gauge the effectiveness and adaptability of the technology in your specific setting. Monitor the results closely and gather feedback from the users.

3. Invest in Training: For any new technology, investing in comprehensive training is crucial. Ensure that your team is not only familiar with how to use the new tools but also understands the safety enhancements they bring. Mobile apps for safety training can be a resource-efficient method to achieve

this, providing on-the-go training that fits into the daily workflow.

4. Regularly Update Safety Protocols: As you integrate new technologies, regularly update your safety protocols to reflect the new tools and techniques at your disposal. This ensures ongoing compliance and maximises the safety benefits of your technological investments.

5. Monitor and Scale: After implementing new technologies, continuously monitor their impact on safety outcomes. Use this data to fine-tune your approach and scale successful technologies across more areas of your operations.

By progressively integrating these technological innovations, you not only enhance worker safety but also streamline operations, making your logistics or warehousing business more efficient and compliant. Remember, the goal is not just to keep up with technology but to leverage it to create a safer, more productive working environment.

6

Navigating Health and Safety Training

"Training is the compass guiding us through the terrain of health and safety, ensuring every step forward is a step toward well-being." – Michelle Obama

Designing Effective Training Programs

When it comes to shaping a robust logistics and warehousing operation, the linchpin to escalating efficiency and ensuring safety lies in the heart of your training programs. You know this, but the real trick is designing these programs in a way that they don't just tick boxes but genuinely enhance skill sets and embed crucial compliance and safety norms within your team. Let's deconstruct this process into digestible chunks: identifying training needs, customising training for various roles, and employing engaging training techniques.

Identifying Training Needs

First things first, understanding the specific training needs of your operation is fundamental. This isn't about implementing a one-size-fits-all approach. Each role in your logistics and warehousing setup could have vastly different requirements. Start with a skills gap analysis. This involves evaluating the skills and knowledge that your current employees possess versus what they need to function optimally. Tools like employee surveys, job analysis, and performance appraisals can serve as your eyes and ears on the ground.

Consider the broader scope too—technological advancements, changes in regulations, and shifts in the market all play into the evolving skill set demands. For instance, with the increasing adoption of automation and AI in logistics, there's a burgeoning need for tech-savvy staff alongside those who can manage and interpret AI outputs.

Once you've pinpointed these needs, prioritise them. Not all training demands immediate attention, and let's be honest, resources are always finite. Focus on what will most significantly impact safety and compliance first, then look at efficiency boosts and other areas.

Customising Training for Various Roles

With your training needs in hand, the next step is tailoring this training to fit the roles within your organisation. The approach for a warehouse operative is likely starkly different from that of a logistics analyst or a truck loader. Each role has unique risks, responsibilities, and requirements.

Start by developing role-specific training modules. For instance, forklift operators need precise instructions on machinery handling and safety protocols, while your IT team might require in-depth training on cybersecurity measures and data compliance. It's not just about what is taught, but how it's taught. The training format might differ—hands-on simulations might benefit operational staff, while classroom-style learning could be more appropriate for managerial roles.

Involve team leaders and existing staff in this process. They can provide insights into the on-the-ground challenges and practical aspects of their roles that you might not see from the top. This collaborative approach not only ensures that the training content is relevant and comprehensive but also aids in buy-in from staff when they see their input valued and incorporated.

Engaging Training Techniques

Now, let's talk about the elephant in the room—no matter how critical the training, if it's not engaging, it's not effective. Adult learners have different motivations and learning styles, and tapping into these can drastically enhance the effectiveness of your training programs.

Interactive learning techniques such as gamification can transform an otherwise dry training session into a dynamic learning experience. Imagine converting compliance training into a competitive game format where employees earn points for each module completed or for passing safety quizzes. This not only makes the learning process enjoyable but also memorable.

Storytelling is another powerful tool. Rather than listing safety protocols in a monotonous PowerPoint, why not use real-life scenarios or case studies that illustrate the consequences of ignoring these protocols? It's about creating an emotional connection with the content that drives the message home.

Don't shy away from technology. E-learning platforms can facilitate a more flexible approach to training, allowing your team to engage with material at their own pace and on their own time. This is particularly advantageous for accommodating the varied schedules within a logistics operation.

Remember, the goal here is not just to inform but to inspire and empower your employees to carry out their roles safely and efficiently. By focusing on engaging training techniques, you ensure that the knowledge sticks and transforms into practical, on-the-job application.

In wrapping up this section of your playbook for navigating health and safety training, remember that the effectiveness of your training programs hinges on their relevance and resonance with your team. By meticulously identifying training needs, customising content for specific roles, and delivering this training in an engaging manner, you set the stage for a safer, more compliant, and efficient operation. And isn't that the ultimate goal?

Certification and Compliance

In the fast-moving world of logistics and warehousing, staying on top of certification and compliance is not just a regulatory necessity; it's a strategic advantage. Keeping your team certified and your operations compliant ensures smooth sailing through regulatory waters, while also safeguarding your reputation and operational integrity.

Mandatory Certifications

First off, let's dive into the sea of mandatory certifications. In the UK, health and safety training isn't just a good idea—it's the law. The Health and Safety at Work etc. Act 1974 is your starting point, mandating that you provide whatever information, instruction, training and supervision necessary to ensure, so far as is reasonably practicable, the health and safety at work of your employees.

This means you'll need to familiarise yourself with a variety of specific training programmes, such as the IOSH Managing Safely for those with a managerial oversight on safety practices, or the NEBOSH National General Certificate in Occupational Health and Safety, which is widely respected by employers in various sectors including warehousing and logistics.

Remember, the type of certification required can vary significantly depending on the specific role and risk associated with it. For instance, operators of heavy machinery such as forklifts are required to have a certified skill set that is periodically updated. Certifications like the RTITB Forklift Operator Training come into play here, ensuring operators are not just competent but also compliant with the latest health and safety regulations.

It's crucial for you, as a leader, to ensure that every member of your team not only starts with the right certification but also maintains and updates their qualifications as needed. This not only keeps you legally compliant but also minimises risk and enhances efficiency in operations.

Keeping Records

Next, let's talk about keeping records. If certifications are the lock, records are the key. They prove your compliance and are your first line of defence in the event of a health and safety inspection or audit. Effective record-keeping involves more than just filing away training certificates; it's an ongoing process that supports the very backbone of your safety culture.

Every training session, every certification gained, and every safety briefing attended should be meticulously recorded and easily accessible. Digital record-keeping systems are particularly useful here, offering searchable databases that can be accessed quickly and remotely—a boon in times of audits or when you need to verify training status on the fly.

An up-to-date training matrix is also an invaluable tool. This should outline who has been trained, in what areas, and when their certifications expire. This not only helps in planning refresher courses but also ensures that no one slips through the net. It's about creating a culture where safety and compliance are as natural as clocking in at the start of the day.

Audit-Readiness

Finally, let's zero in on audit-readiness. Think of it as not just being ready but being confident that you can handle an audit at any given time. Audits, whether internal or external, are a fact of life in the logistics and warehousing sector. They are rigorous, often unannounced, and they demand instant access to detailed compliance records.

Audit-readiness starts with a culture of compliance. This means regular training updates, refresher courses, and spontaneous compliance checks that keep everyone on their toes. Encourage your managers to conduct regular 'mini-audits', reviewing safety protocols and compliance records as part of their routine. This not only prepares your team for the real thing but also helps to engrain compliance into your operational DNA.

Preparation also involves simulating audit scenarios. Use these simulations to stress-test your record-keeping systems and compliance protocols. Where are the gaps? How quickly can you retrieve and present required documentation? How robust are your safety practices under scrutiny? This kind of proactive approach can turn a potentially stressful audit into just another day at the office.

Compliance isn't just about ticking boxes. It's about building a safe, efficient, and legally compliant operation that stands up to scrutiny and sets a benchmark in the logistics and warehousing industry. By focusing on rigorous certification, meticulous record-keeping, and constant audit-readiness, you're not just complying with the law—you're setting the stage for operational excellence. Remember, in the world of logistics and warehousing, being compliant is not just about avoiding penalties; it's about creating an environment where safety and efficiency drive your success.

Advanced Training Techniques

When it comes to health and safety training in the logistics and warehousing sector, sticking to traditional methods might seem like the path of least resistance. However, embracing advanced training techniques can significantly enhance the effectiveness of your training programmes, ensuring that they are not only comprehensive but also engaging and impactful. Let's dive into some of the most effective advanced training techniques that you, as a senior manager or director, can incorporate to elevate your team's performance and compliance.

Simulation-Based Training

Imagine being able to expose your team to real-world scenarios without the risks associated with actual on-the-job experiences. Simulation-based training allows you to create such an environment where your employees can learn to handle complex situations in a controlled, virtual setting. This method is particularly beneficial in logistics and warehousing, where the cost of errors can be high—both in terms of finance and safety.

By using simulation tools, you can craft scenarios tailored to your specific operational challenges. Whether it's managing a sudden influx of inventory, dealing with equipment failure, or navigating a hazardous material spill, simulations can prepare your team for almost anything. The key here is realism—the more realistic your scenarios, the better prepared your team will be when they face similar challenges in the real world.

Moreover, simulation-based training is not just about handling physical goods. It can also be used for soft skills development, such as team leadership and decision-making under pressure. These are crucial for ensuring that safety protocols are followed diligently and that your team can respond swiftly and effectively to any unexpected challenges.

Virtual Reality (VR) Applications

Taking simulation a step further, VR applications in training can revolutionise how your team engages with and retains crucial safety information. By donning a VR headset, employees can immerse themselves in lifelike scenarios that require them to navigate their way through various challenges, all while adhering to safety protocols.

The immersive nature of VR means that it's not just a visual experience; it's a full-body and mind engagement that helps in forming muscle memory and decision-making skills in a risk-free environment. For example, using VR to simulate the experience of operating a high-reach forklift in a crowded warehouse can train employees on safe operation techniques without the risk of actual accidents.

Another advantage of VR is its ability to track user performance meticulously. This data can be invaluable for identifying areas where an individual might need more focus or additional training, allowing you to customise learning paths for enhanced safety outcomes.

Feedback and Assessment Tools

No training programme is complete without a mechanism to evaluate its effectiveness, and this is where feedback and assessment tools come into play. Advanced training techniques often incorporate sophisticated analytics that can provide detailed insights into employee performance both during and after training sessions.

Consider integrating systems that allow for real-time feedback during training exercises. This can include digital checklists, mobile apps for instant responses, and even AI-driven analysis tools that measure decision-making processes and reaction times. The immediate feedback helps trainees to correct their actions on the spot, reinforcing the learning process.

Post-training assessments, on the other hand, should help you gauge not just what your team members have learned, but also how well they can apply their knowledge in real-world situations. Tools like digital quizzes, scenario-based assessments, and even peer reviews can be valuable here. These assessments should be designed to not only test knowledge but also to evaluate behavioural and procedural adherence which are critical in maintaining safety standards in your operations.

Additionally, consider longitudinal studies of training outcomes to truly measure the impact of your training over time. This could involve follow-up assessments weeks or months after the initial training, to see how well skills and knowledge have been retained and applied. This long-term data can help you refine and adjust your training programmes for even better results in the future.

By incorporating these advanced training techniques into your health and safety programmes, you not only enhance the learning experience but also significantly boost the overall safety and efficiency of your operations. Remember, the goal is to not just comply with necessary regulations but to create a proactive culture of safety and excellence in your workplace. Through simulation-based training, VR applications, and robust feedback mechanisms, you equip your team with the skills and knowledge they need to thrive in a demanding and dynamic industry.

RECAP AND ACTION ITEMS

Congratulations on reaching the end of this crucial chapter on Navigating Health and Safety Training. You're now armed with the knowledge to design effective training programmes, maintain compliance with certifications, and employ advanced training techniques like VR and simulations. Let's consolidate this into actionable steps that you can implement to enhance safety and efficiency in your operations.

First, take a moment to thoroughly assess your current training programmes. Are they truly tailored to the specific needs of various roles within your organisation? Remember, a one-size-fits-all approach rarely covers all bases effectively. Identifying gaps in your current training can lead to more targeted and engaging sessions. Engage with your team leaders and HR department to pinpoint these needs and start crafting more customised training plans.

Next, streamline your certification and compliance processes. Are your records up to date and easily accessible? If not, consider digitising these records to enhance traceability and ease of access. This will not only prepare you for audits but will also reduce the administrative burden on your staff, allowing them to focus more on operational excellence rather than paperwork.

Lastly, embrace the technological advancements available today. If you haven't already, integrating simulation-based training and VR can revolutionise how your team learns, making training more interactive and memorable. Additionally, invest in sophisticated feedback and assessment tools to measure the effectiveness of your training programmes accurately. This data will be invaluable in refining your approaches and ensuring that your team is not just compliant, but also competent and confident in their roles.

By taking these steps, you will not only ensure the safety and compliance of your operations but also encourage a culture of continuous improvement and innovation within your team. Remember, in the fast-evolving sector of logistics and warehousing, staying ahead means being proactive about training and development. Now, go forth and put these insights into action. Your team, and your bottom line, will thank you for it.

7

Health and Safety in the Transport Yard Environment

"An ounce of prevention is worth a pound of cure." – Benjamin Franklin

Safety Requirements for Visiting Drivers

Navigating the bustling ecosystem of a transport yard can be quite the ballet. With vehicles big and small zipping about, safety isn't just another box to tick—it's your lifeline. As a transport manager, ensuring that every driver who sets foot in your yard is well-versed in safety protocols is crucial, not just for their wellbeing but also for the smooth operation of your hub. So, let's break it down into digestible chunks: Orientation and Information, Personal Protective Equipment (PPE), and Safety Procedures for Unfamiliar Environments.

Orientation and Information

First impressions matter, and the initial orientation is the cornerstone of safety for visiting drivers. Think of it as the map that guides them through the labyrinth of logistical operations. Every driver stepping into your yard should be equipped with the necessary information that acquaints them with the layout and safety protocols of the site.

Start with a comprehensive briefing session. This isn't just about handing over a pamphlet or showing a generic safety video. Tailor these sessions to address the specific risks and rules of your yard. Use interactive tools like digital maps or virtual tours that can help drivers visualise the environment they will be navigating. It's about making the unfamiliar familiar, quickly and effectively.

Incorporate a sign-in procedure that logs their entry and ensures that they've received all necessary safety information. This log can be a lifesaver in ensuring compliance and can serve as a legal safeguard should any incidents occur.

Remember, clear communication is key. Ensure all signs around the yard are up to date and legible, with necessary warnings and directions clearly marked. Language barriers can pose significant risks, so provide multilingual support in your orientations and signage where possible. This ensures that every driver, no matter where they're from, has the information needed to navigate your yard safely.

Personal Protective Equipment (PPE)

Next up, let's talk gear—specifically, Personal Protective Equipment (PPE). In the whirlwind of activity that defines a transport yard, the right PPE can mean the difference between a normal day at work and a trip to the emergency room.

The baseline here is high-visibility clothing. Every visiting driver should be kitted out in high-vis vests or jackets. These are non-negotiable, as they ensure that drivers are seen by operators of heavy machinery and other vehicles, especially in areas of the yard where visibility might be compromised.

Footwear is another critical element. Safety boots with steel toes and slip-resistant soles are essential. They protect against a myriad of risks, from heavy objects falling onto the feet to slips on oily or wet surfaces.

Don't forget about head protection. Hard hats should be mandatory in areas where there's a risk of falling objects or where drivers might bump their heads against machinery.

Providing a PPE station at the entrance of your yard where drivers can gear up before entering can streamline the process. Ensure this station is well-stocked and that all equipment is in good repair. Remember, worn-out PPE won't offer much protection.

Safety Procedures for Unfamiliar Environments

Even the most seasoned driver can find themselves at sea in a new or unfamiliar yard. This section is all about turning the unknown into a well-trodden path with clear, actionable safety procedures.

Start with vehicle movement guidelines. Every yard will have its own traffic flow and rules. Make these rules second nature for visiting drivers through clear, concise guidelines provided during the orientation. Highlight areas where special caution is needed, like busy crossroads within the yard or zones with pedestrian traffic.

Emergency procedures are crucial. Every driver should know what to do in case of different types of emergencies, be it a fire, a chemical spill, or a severe weather event. Drill down on the locations of emergency exits and assembly points, and ensure these are well-marked and communicated during the initial briefing.

Lastly, address the human element. Encourage a culture where drivers feel comfortable asking questions if they're unsure about the safety procedures.

Set up a buddy system where a visiting driver is paired with an experienced yard operator during their first few visits. This not only boosts safety but also fosters a sense of community and support.

By breaking down the safety requirements into these focused areas, you not only safeguard the visiting drivers but also enhance the overall efficiency and safety of your transport yard. Remember, a safe yard is a productive yard.

Vehicle and Equipment Safety Protocols - Vehicle Movements and Control

In the bustling environment of a transport yard, overseeing the safe movement of vehicles is not just a recommendation—it's an absolute necessity. You, as a transport manager, are the linchpin in the smooth operation of vehicle logistics, and how you manage this can significantly mitigate risks.

Firstly, it's crucial to establish clear traffic routes. Every driver, whether they're a seasoned regular or a first-time visitor, should be clear on where they can and cannot go. Signage plays a big role here. It's not just about slapping up a few 'keep out' signs here and there. Think about using large, clear markers that can be seen over the top of a loaded lorry. Implement one-way systems wherever possible to reduce the risks of collisions and confusion.

Speed limits must be strictly enforced. Remember, a transport yard is not a racetrack. Speeding increases the likelihood of accidents exponentially. Implementing radar speed signs can act as a deterrent, as well as regular reminders during driver briefings.

Another aspect you'll want to tighten up on is vehicle access controls. This means controlling who gets in and out of the yard. Automated gate systems can help manage this effectively, ensuring that only authorised personnel are moving in and out of the yard, thus keeping trespassers at bay and reducing theft or vandalism.

Training is another pivotal element. Every driver should undergo a yard-specific orientation that covers all key safety aspects, including vehicle movements. Consider simulations or practical demonstrations as part of this training to ensure drivers understand the protocols in a hands-on manner.

Lastly, the use of spotters can be incredibly beneficial, especially in larger yards where blind spots may be more common. These individuals can help guide drivers when backing up or navigating tight spaces, significantly reducing the risk of an accident.

Coupling and Uncoupling Procedures

Coupling and uncoupling trailers are tasks that might seem straightforward but are fraught with potential hazards if not done correctly. As a transport manager, ensuring that these procedures are carried out safely is a critical part of your role.

Start with a standardised checklist. Before any coupling or uncoupling activity, drivers should complete a pre-operation inspection. This checklist should cover the condition of the coupling devices, brake connections, electrical connectors, and the landing gear. Ensuring that everything is in good working order before beginning the process can prevent a multitude of problems.

Training, again, is indispensable. It's not enough for drivers to know what needs to be done; they must also understand how to react if something goes wrong. Regular training sessions, accompanied by refresher courses, will ensure that all personnel are up to speed with the best practices and latest safety protocols.

During the coupling process, ensure the trailer is properly supported. This might sound obvious, but accidents still occur due to negligence in this area. Use wheel chocks to secure the trailer and ensure that the landing gear is fully lowered and locked.

Visibility is key during coupling and uncoupling. Yard lighting should be sufficient to illuminate work areas clearly to avoid mishaps that are attributable to poor lighting conditions. Consider investing in motion-sensor lights that illuminate areas as vehicles and drivers approach, enhancing safety especially during early mornings or late evenings.

Loading and Unloading Safety

The loading and unloading process is inherently risky, with potential for injury or damage if mishandled. Implementing rigorous safety protocols here is non-negotiable.

First off, vehicle stability is paramount. Ensure that lorries are parked on level ground during loading and unloading. The handbrake should always be engaged, and, where applicable, wheel chocks used to prevent the vehicle from moving.

Communication is critical during loading and unloading. Use walkie-talkies or other communication devices to ensure that everyone involved in the process is in sync. The loader operator, the driver, and the ground personnel should be in constant communication to coordinate their actions.

Load security is another crucial area. Improperly secured loads can shift during transport, leading to damaged goods or even accidents. All loads should be evenly distributed and securely fastened. Regular inspections and audits of loading procedures can help ensure compliance with safety standards.

Automation and mechanical aids can greatly enhance safety in loading operations. Forklifts, pallet jacks, and conveyor belts reduce the need for manual handling, which in turn minimises the risk of physical injury. However, ensure that all personnel operating such machinery are properly trained and certified.

Lastly, emergency procedures should be clearly established and communicated. In the event of an accident or emergency during loading or unloading, it is crucial that all personnel know exactly what to do. Regular drills and the clear marking of emergency exits and assembly points will help prepare your team for any eventuality.

By meticulously managing these aspects of vehicle and equipment safety protocols, you not only ensure the smooth running of operations but also safeguard the health and well-being of every individual entering your transport yard. This proactive approach to safety can significantly reduce the risk of costly accidents and injuries, fostering a culture of vigilance and compliance that resonates throughout your operations.

Yard Maintenance and Emergency Procedures

Managing a transport yard effectively hinges on maintaining a safe, efficient, and prepared environment. This requires a vigilant approach to yard maintenance and a robust strategy for handling emergencies. Let's dive into the nuts and bolts of keeping your yard in top shape and ensuring you're prepared for any mishaps.

Combustible Material Management

In the hustle of daily operations, it's easy to overlook the risks posed by improperly stored combustible materials. However, the potential for fire is a critical risk in transport yards, where fuels, oils, and other flammable substances are commonplace.

Firstly, you need to identify all combustible materials present in your yard. This includes checking not just the obvious — like fuel — but also packaging materials, waste products, and even the vehicles themselves. Once identified, these materials must be stored safely. Fuels, for instance, should be kept in clearly labelled, purpose-built containers away from general traffic areas and ignition sources.

The layout of your storage areas is crucial. Ensure there is sufficient space between combustible materials and other storage items to prevent any accidental fires from spreading. Moreover, your yard should have clear signage indicating no-smoking zones and other fire hazard areas, especially near storage points.

Implementing regular checks and balances is another vital step. Routine inspections can help identify potential risks before they escalate into real threats. These inspections should be documented meticulously, creating a trail of compliance should you need to demonstrate your proactive management to insurers or regulatory bodies.

Lastly, training your staff on the risks associated with combustible materials and the correct handling procedures cannot be overstated. They should know how to manage spills, dispose of combustible waste properly, and what to do in case of a fire. This knowledge not only helps prevent incidents but also ensures a swift and effective response if an emergency occurs.

Yard Safety Inspections and Maintenance

Keeping your yard safe is an ongoing process, demanding regular inspections and maintenance. This proactive approach not only helps prevent accidents but also boosts operational efficiency by ensuring that equipment and vehicles are in good working condition.

Start with a comprehensive inspection schedule covering all areas of the yard. This includes checking road surfaces for potholes or cracks, ensuring that signage is clear and unobstructed, and verifying that all barriers and fences are secure and intact. It's also essential to inspect lighting to ensure that all areas of the yard are well-lit, as poor lighting can be a significant hazard, particularly during winter months.

Maintenance tasks should be prioritised based on the risk they pose. For example, any issues that could potentially cause a vehicle accident should be addressed as a matter of urgency. This could include repairing damaged road surfaces or replacing faulty lighting.

Record-keeping is your best friend here. Maintain logs of all inspections, noting any issues found and actions taken. This not only helps you track your maintenance schedule but also proves compliance with health and safety regulations.

Engaging your team in these inspections can be beneficial. They often have first-hand knowledge of any emerging issues and can provide valuable insights into areas that might be overlooked during more formal checks.

Accident Reporting and Risk Management

No matter how comprehensive your safety protocols are, accidents can still happen. Effective risk management and a clear accident reporting procedure are essential components of yard management.

First, ensure that all employees know how to report an accident. This includes not only major incidents but also near-misses, which can provide crucial information for preventing more serious accidents in the future. Reporting procedures should be straightforward and accessible to all staff members, possibly through multiple channels like in-person reporting, digital forms, or a dedicated hotline.

Once an accident is reported, it's crucial to act swiftly. Immediate actions might include administering first aid, containing any hazards, or notifying emergency services if necessary. Every incident, no matter how minor, should be followed up with a thorough investigation to determine its cause and what can be done to prevent a recurrence. This might involve revisiting risk assessments, updating protocols, or increasing training.

Part of managing risks in a dynamic environment like a transport yard includes regular review and update of your risk assessments. As operations change, new equipment is introduced, or new safety information becomes available, your risk management strategies should evolve too. This ensures that you are always several steps ahead in managing potential hazards.

By maintaining a rigorous approach to yard maintenance, staying vigilant about combustible materials, conducting regular inspections, and fostering a robust culture of safety and compliance, you create not just a safer workplace but also a more efficient and resilient operation. Remember, a well-maintained yard is the backbone of safe and successful transport management.

RECAP AND ACTION ITEMS

Navigating the complexities of health and safety in a transport yard isn't just about compliance; it's about creating a culture of safety that permeates every aspect of operations. You've now equipped yourself with essential guidelines spanning from the induction of visiting drivers to the meticulous maintenance of the yard itself.

Let's start with ensuring every visiting driver who enters your yard knows exactly what's expected of them. The orientation process should be thorough yet straightforward, ensuring all safety information is communicated effectively. Here's your first action: Review your current driver orientation materials. Could a new driver understand and apply the information easily? If not, it's time for a revamp.

Next, consider the personal protective equipment (PPE) you require in your yard. It's one thing to have rules, but are they being followed consistently? Conduct random checks to ensure compliance and understand where gaps might exist. Additionally, consider investing in signage that reminds everyone of the PPE requirements as they enter specific zones within your yard.

Moving on to vehicle and equipment safety, your action here is to supervise and periodically review the procedures for vehicle movements, coupling, and uncoupling, as well as loading and unloading. These are high-risk activities that can lead to significant accidents if not managed properly. Consider implementing a refresher training session that addresses these key areas and tests the practical knowledge of your team.

For yard maintenance, your focus should be on proactive risk management. Schedule regular inspections and create a checklist that covers all aspects of the yard, including the management of combustible materials. Ensure that these inspections are documented and that any issues identified are addressed promptly.

Lastly, an effective accident reporting system is pivotal. It not only helps in dealing with incidents more efficiently but also aids in preventing future occurrences. Review your current accident reporting process. Is it straightforward? Are your staff trained on what constitutes an 'incident' and how to report it? Make sure there's a clear, accessible way for employees to report risks and incidents.

By taking these steps, you're not just ticking off boxes on a compliance checklist. You're leading by example and fostering a safety-first culture that protects your team, your equipment, and your business. Remember, a safe yard is an efficient yard.

8

Legal Compliance and Beyond

"In matters of style, swim with the current; in matters of principle, stand like a rock." - Thomas Jefferson

Staying Ahead of Regulatory Changes

Navigating the labyrinthine realm of regulatory changes in logistics and warehousing can often feel like trying to catch smoke: elusive and ever-changing. Yet, as you're well aware, staying ahead isn't just about compliance; it's about gaining a competitive edge. Let's break down the strategies that can keep you not just afloat, but ahead.

Monitoring Legal Updates

Keeping up with legal updates is akin to maintaining a high-performance engine; it requires constant attention and fine-tuning. In the fast-paced world of logistics, being the last to know can cost you not just in terms of compliance, but also in operational efficiency and reputation.

Firstly, consider the digital tools and resources at your disposal. Regulatory technology solutions can automate the tracking of legal changes. These systems not only alert you to relevant updates but can also help in assessing the impact on your operations. Investing in such technology is no longer a luxury but a necessity, especially when considering the volume and frequency of regulatory updates.

Another key strategy is to encourage relationships with legal experts who specialise in logistics and warehousing. These professionals can provide insights that are not immediately obvious from the plain language of new legislation. They can translate legal jargon into actionable advice, ensuring that you're not just compliant, but also ahead of the curve.

Lastly, create a culture of compliance within your organisation. When your team understands the importance of regulatory changes, they can better support compliance efforts. Regular training sessions and updates can equip them to handle new regulations effectively. Remember, compliance is not just the responsibility of your legal team; it's a company-wide endeavour.

Impact of Brexit on Regulations

Brexit has reshuffled the deck in terms of regulatory compliance, with significant ramifications for logistics and warehousing. The separation from the EU means that you must now navigate a dual regulatory environment: one for operations within the UK and another for those involving the EU.

First off, you need to stay informed about the new UK-specific regulations that are replacing or modifying the existing EU directives. This is particularly pertinent in areas such as customs, safety standards, and environmental regulations. Understanding these changes will help you adjust your business model to meet the new requirements.

Moreover, consider the longer-term strategic adjustments. For instance, Brexit might change your supply chain design, necessitating a shift in your warehousing locations or logistics routes. These changes might not only be about compliance but optimising for cost, speed, and reliability in a new economic landscape.

Engaging with logistic and warehousing associations can also provide insights and support. These bodies often have firsthand information from negotiations and regulatory developments. They can offer guidance and advocacy that helps you navigate the Brexit-induced changes more smoothly.

Engaging with Industry Bodies

Collaboration is key in staying proactive about regulatory changes. Industry bodies and associations play a pivotal role here. They not only provide a collective voice but also a reservoir of resources that can help you anticipate and adapt to changes.

Membership in relevant bodies such as the UK Warehousing Association (UKWA) or the Chartered Institute of Logistics and Transport (CILT) offers numerous benefits. These organisations often have access to early warnings about regulatory shifts and can provide bespoke advice on compliance. They also offer networking opportunities with peers who may have innovative solutions to shared challenges.

Participation in forums and committees can also amplify your influence over regulatory changes. By being part of the conversation, you can help shape the regulations that will govern your industry. This is not just about defence but about crafting a regulatory environment that encourages growth and innovation in your sector.

Moreover, these bodies often conduct training and certification programs that can ensure your team remains skilled and informed. Encouraging your staff to engage in continuous professional development through these channels not only helps in compliance but also boosts morale and retention.

In conclusion, staying ahead of regulatory changes requires a multifaceted approach: leveraging technology for monitoring updates, understanding the implications of Brexit, and engaging actively with industry bodies. By adopting these strategies, you ensure that your logistics and warehousing operations are not just compliant but also competitively poised in a shifting regulatory landscape.

Handling Inspections and Audits

Preparing for HSE Inspections

When the Health and Safety Executive (HSE) comes knocking, it's not just about passing the test; it's about acing it. Think of HSE inspections as an opportunity to showcase the robustness of your logistics and warehousing operations. To ensure you're not just compliant but also exemplary, preparation is key.

Start with a rigorous audit of your current practices. This isn't about ticking boxes; it's about integrating safety into the DNA of your operations. Ensure that all your equipment meets the latest safety standards and that safety notices are both visible and up-to-date. Remember, an informed team is an empowered team. Regular training sessions that do more than just go through the motions are essential. They should breathe life into your safety protocols, ensuring that every team member understands their role in maintaining a safe work environment.

Document everything. In the age of digital dominance, paper trails haven't lost their relevance. Ensure that your records are meticulous and easily accessible. This includes maintenance logs, training records, and incident reports. When an inspector asks for these, pulling them up promptly will not only demonstrate your organisational skills but also your commitment to transparency and safety.

Mock inspections can be a game-changer. They keep your team alert and prepared for unexpected visits. Use them as a drill sergeant would, to keep your troops in inspection-ready shape at all times. This proactive approach can transform potentially stressful inspections into affirmations of your company's dedication to safety.

Effective Response Strategies

The day has arrived, and the inspector walks through your doors. How you respond in the next few hours can significantly influence the outcome of this visit. First impressions count, so meet and greet the inspector professionally and cordially. Establishing a positive tone from the get-go can set the stage for a constructive dialogue.

Have a designated point person. This should be someone who is not only knowledgeable about your operations but also calm under pressure. They will act as the liaison between your team and the inspector, ensuring that communications are clear and that no question goes unanswered.

Be transparent. If an issue is identified, don't skirt around it. Acknowledge it, and more importantly, outline the steps you've already taken or plan to take to rectify it. Inspectors will appreciate honesty and a proactive attitude towards solving problems.

Keep the inspector informed about your safety protocols and how they are integrated into daily operations. Walk them through the processes, emphasising not just compliance but how these measures contribute to a safer and more efficient working environment. This demonstrates not only adherence to legal requirements but also a commitment to continuous improvement.

Corrective Actions Post-Audit

Once the inspector has left, the real work begins. Whether the feedback was glowing or came with a list of recommendations, your response remains crucial. Immediate, medium, and long-term action plans should be developed to address any issues raised. This shows ongoing commitment to excellence and prevents the recurrence of similar issues in future audits.

For issues requiring immediate attention, assemble a task force to tackle these as swiftly as possible. Quick responses reflect well on your company's dedication to safety and compliance.

For more systemic issues, consider forming a review committee to delve deeper. This committee can analyse why the issue arose in the first place and what systemic changes might be necessary to prevent a recurrence. This might involve revising training programmes, updating or acquiring new equipment, or even rethinking certain operational protocols.

Finally, integrate the lessons learned into your standard operating procedures. Training should be updated to include these learnings, ensuring that the same mistakes are not repeated. Consider sharing these experiences in workshops or seminars. Not only does this reinforce the importance of compliance within your team, but it also helps in building a culture of transparency and continuous improvement.

In the dynamic field of logistics and warehousing, staying ahead in terms of compliance and safety isn't just about adhering to the rules. It's about setting new standards and continuously pushing the boundaries to ensure operations are not just efficient but are also safe and sustainable. Remember, every inspection is an opportunity to learn and improve, turning potential challenges into showcases of your company's commitment to excellence.

Ethical Considerations

Beyond Compliance

Let's dive into what might initially appear as the softer side of business - ethics. Yet, in reality, it's anything but soft. Ethical business practices form the bedrock of your company's reputation and longevity. You know as well as I do that compliance isn't just about ticking boxes. It's about setting a standard that goes beyond the basic legal requirements.

Consider this: when you choose to operate beyond compliance, you're investing in a level of operational excellence that not only minimises risk but also enhances your company's standing. It's about being seen not just as a company that does things right, but as a company that does the right things.

So, how do you ensure that your logistics or warehousing operation excels ethically? Start with transparency. Be clear about your methods, your sourcing, and your labour practices. This openness not only builds trust with your clients and stakeholders but also sets a clear expectation for your team's conduct.

Next, think about the long-term impacts of your decisions. Short-term gains should not compromise long-term sustainability. For instance, cutting corners to meet immediate logistical demands might save time or money now, but what will be the cost in terms of safety incidents or damaged reputation later?

By encouraging an environment where ethical decisions are valued and rewarded, you create a culture that naturally aligns with high compliance and operational standards. Remember, ethical considerations are not just about avoiding bad decisions but about actively making good ones.

Corporate Social Responsibility (CSR)

Now, let's shift gears to Corporate Social Responsibility or CSR, which is increasingly becoming a non-negotiable part of business strategy, particularly in logistics and warehousing. CSR goes beyond compliance by embedding social, environmental, and economic concerns into your business operations.

You might wonder, "How can CSR apply specifically to my sector?" Quite directly, actually. For example, consider the environmental impact of your logistics operations. Are you implementing green technologies or practices that reduce your carbon footprint? Are you using resources efficiently? Sustainability is a huge part of CSR and can significantly influence your public image.

Moreover, CSR can help you engage better with the communities you operate in. This might be through supporting local employment, improving infrastructure, or sponsoring educational initiatives. Such engagements not only enhance your company's image but also build meaningful relationships with the community, potentially smoothing over any operational frictions.

Financially, integrating CSR can lead to efficiencies that might reduce costs in the long run. For instance, investing in energy-efficient warehousing can reduce utility bills, and using a well-planned logistics network can minimise fuel consumption.

It's essential to communicate your CSR activities clearly and regularly. Transparency in your CSR initiatives reassures stakeholders of your commitment to ethical practices and can lead to increased investor confidence and customer loyalty.

Ethical Supply Chain Management

Finally, let's tackle Ethical Supply Chain Management. In the logistics and warehousing industry, your supply chain is not just a network of companies but a reflection of your business values. The ethical management of your supply chain is crucial for maintaining compliance and ensuring overall business integrity.

Start by assessing your suppliers and partners. Do they follow labour laws? Are their business practices environmentally sound? Conducting regular audits and insisting on transparency from your suppliers can help you maintain an ethical supply chain.

But it's not just about monitoring. It's also about collaboration. Work with your suppliers to improve their practices. Sometimes, suppliers might lack the resources or knowledge to meet the required standards. By providing training or resources, you help elevate their operations, which in turn strengthens your supply chain.

Another aspect to consider is the risk of modern slavery, which unfortunately still exists and can be hidden within complex supply chains. Implementing thorough checks and maintaining a zero-tolerance policy towards any form of forced labour is not only ethically sound but also aligns with legal standards like the UK Modern Slavery Act.

Ethical supply chain management also involves dealing with unexpected ethical dilemmas. For example, what do you do if you discover a long-term supplier suddenly engages in questionable practices? Deciding whether to cut ties immediately or to help them adjust their practices is a tough but necessary consideration.

In conclusion, weaving ethical considerations into the fabric of your business operations isn't just about building a good image. It's about creating a sustainable and resilient business that stands the test of time and fluctuating markets. As you continue to navigate the complexities of the logistics and warehousing industry, remember that your ethical choices define not just what your company does, but who you are as leaders

RECAP AND ACTION ITEMS

Navigating the complex web of logistics and warehousing compliance isn't just about sticking to the rules; it's about setting a benchmark in the industry. You've explored various facets—from staying proactive with regulatory changes post-Brexit to managing inspections and encouraging an ethical work environment. Let's boil down this knowledge into actionable steps that you, as a leader in this field, can implement right away.

1. Set Up a Regulatory Alert System: If you haven't already, establish a mechanism to stay updated with legal changes. This could be as simple as subscribing to industry newsletters or as sophisticated as implementing regulatory tracking software. The key here is consistency and immediacy, ensuring you're always the first to know and react.

2. Engage Proactively with Industry Bodies: Make it a part of your quarterly agenda to engage with these bodies, not just for insights but also to influence policy-making. Your active participation can shape the regulations that will govern your operations.

3. Brexit Action Plan: Given the ongoing shifts post-Brexit, assign a dedicated team to specifically monitor how changes affect your operations and compliance requirements. This team should report directly to you with actionable insights and recommendations.

4. Simulate Inspections: Regularly scheduled mock inspections can dramatically improve your team's readiness for real ones. Use these simulations to streamline your responses and tighten any operational loopholes. Ensure

that learning and feedback from these are integrated back into training and processes.

5. Audit Review Meetings: After every audit, hold a review meeting that not only discusses the findings but also maps out a clear plan for corrective actions. Timeliness in addressing these issues is crucial, so set deadlines and assign clear responsibilities.

6. Champion Corporate Social Responsibility: Let CSR be more than a compliance requirement. Embed it into your business strategy and company culture. Initiatives could range from environmental sustainability to community engagement—actions that reflect your company's values and ethics.

7. Ethical Supply Chain Audits: Go beyond the minimum standards and regularly evaluate your supply chain practices for ethical considerations. This shouldn't be seen as an audit but as a continuous commitment to maintaining a clean, fair, and sustainable supply chain.

Implementing these steps will not only ensure compliance but also position your company as a leader in ethical business practices and operational excellence. In logistics and warehousing, staying ahead isn't just about moving goods efficiently but moving them responsibly. Remember, in this rapidly evolving landscape, being proactive is better than being reactive.

9

Health and Safety Metrics and Reporting

"An incident is just the tip of the iceberg, a sign of a much larger problem below the surface." – Don Brown

Key Performance Indicators (KPIs)

When you're at the helm of logistics and warehousing operations, the clarity of your vision depends significantly on the quality of the metrics you track. Just as a seasoned captain needs precise instruments to navigate turbulent seas, you need the right Key Performance Indicators (KPIs) to steer your organisation through the complex world of supply chain management. Let's explore how you can select, track, and report these KPIs effectively.

Selecting Relevant KPIs

Choosing the right KPIs is not just about picking metrics that look good on paper; it's about finding indicators that resonate with the core objectives of your logistics and warehousing operations. These indicators should give you a clear line of sight into performance areas that directly impact your strategic goals.

Start by identifying what success looks like for your operations. Is it faster delivery times, lower incident rates, or higher customer satisfaction? Once you have this mapped out, you can begin to select KPIs that align with these goals. For instance, if reducing the accident rate is a priority, you might monitor metrics such as 'Days Without an Incident' or 'Incident Severity Rate'.

However, it's crucial to strike a balance. While it's tempting to track a wide array of metrics, too many KPIs can dilute focus and make it challenging to discern what's truly important. Aim for KPIs that are S.M.A.R.T: Specific, Measurable, Achievable, Relevant, and Time-bound. This approach ensures that each KPI holds specific value to your objectives and isn't just noise.

Consider also the interplay between different KPIs. In the intricate dance of logistics, metrics often influence one another. For example, efforts to speed up delivery times shouldn't lead to an increase in safety incidents. Hence, your KPIs need to be balanced to promote a holistic approach to performance improvement.

Tracking and Analysis

Now that you've selected your KPIs, the next step is tracking them. But let's be honest, data collection can be as tedious as watching paint dry, yet it's just as fundamental. The key here is not just collecting data, but collecting the right data at the right time.

Implement systems that automate data collection as much as possible. Technology like RFID tags and GPS tracking can provide real-time data feeds that are both accurate and timely. Moreover, integrating these systems with your existing ERP or warehouse management software can help you capture a comprehensive data set without adding extra steps to your team's workflow.

Once the data is in, the analysis begins. This is where the magic happens, turning raw data into actionable insights. Data visualisation tools can be incredibly powerful here, helping to spot trends and outliers at a glance. Whether it's a sudden spike in delivery delays or an unusual decrease in stock discrepancies, visual tools help you quickly zero in on areas that need attention.

However, the analysis should not just be about spotting problems. It's equally important to identify what's working well so you can replicate these successes across other areas of your operations. Regularly scheduled reviews with your team can encourage a culture of continuous improvement, turning KPI tracking into a proactive, rather than reactive, process.

Reporting to Stakeholders

Finally, we come to the art of reporting. In the world of logistics and warehousing, where operations are as visible as the proverbial iceberg (with much hidden beneath the surface), effective reporting can illuminate your achievements and challenges alike.

The key to effective KPI reporting is clarity and relevance. Reports should be tailored to their audience. For instance, while senior management might require detailed reports on all KPIs, other stakeholders like investors might only need an overview focusing on KPIs related to financial performance and risk management.

Utilise dashboards and scorecards that summarise data and highlight trends, making it easy for stakeholders to digest information quickly. Remember, the goal of reporting is not just to inform but to engage. By providing clear and concise KPI reports, you can help stakeholders understand the challenges and appreciate the successes of your operations.

Moreover, regular reporting creates a rhythm of accountability in your team. It sets a recurring deadline for evaluating performance and implementing improvements, which can significantly enhance the dynamics of your operations.

By following these guidelines in selecting, tracking, and reporting KPIs, you not only gain a deeper understanding of your operations but also equip yourself with the tools to navigate the complexities of the logistics and warehousing landscape more effectively. As these processes become second nature, you'll find that your role as a leader is not just about managing what you can see but also about illuminating what you can't.

Incident Reporting and Investigation

Systems for Incident Reporting

In the dynamic environment of logistics and warehousing, incidents are, unfortunately, a part of life. However, the true measure of your leadership is not necessarily the number of incidents, but how they are reported and managed. Establishing a robust system for incident reporting is foundational in maintaining not just compliance, but also in encouraging a culture of safety and continuous improvement.

Firstly, consider the accessibility of your reporting system. It's crucial that all employees, regardless of their role or the shift they work, can report incidents effortlessly. Digital platforms can offer an intuitive solution here, allowing real-time reporting through various devices. This immediacy not only speeds up the response times but also enhances the accuracy of the incident data captured.

Moreover, your system should assure anonymity and protection to those reporting. This feature encourages a more open communication line, where employees feel secure to report minor incidents or near misses that could be crucial learning points. Remember, the goal is to capture as much data as possible - not to encourage a blame culture.

Integration with other data systems can exponentially increase the value of your incident reports. Linking incident data with HR records, for example, can help you track if specific training programmes correlate with a decrease in incident rates. Similarly, connecting this data to your operational schedules might reveal if certain times or shifts tend to have higher incident rates, thus allowing for more targeted interventions.

Conducting Effective Investigations

Once an incident is reported, the next crucial step is the investigation process. Effective investigations go beyond determining what happened; they explore why it happened and how similar incidents can be prevented in the future. This process should not be a fault-finding mission but a truth-seeking one that promotes a safer workplace.

Begin with assembling the right investigation team. This team should ideally be a mix of individuals from various levels within your organisation, including those directly involved in the incident and those who can provide an unbiased perspective. In some cases, it might be beneficial to include external experts, particularly where specialised knowledge of machinery or processes is required.

The methodology of the investigation should be systematic and structured. Start by securing the incident scene and collecting initial statements and evidence before they can be tampered with or memories fade. Use tools such as the '5 Whys' technique to drill down to the root cause. This method involves asking 'Why?' successively until you reach the underlying cause, which often is not immediately apparent.

Documenting every step of the investigation is crucial. Not only does this serve as a record for future reference, but it also ensures the process is transparent and actionable items are followed up on. Digital tools can be particularly useful here, providing templates and workflows that ensure consistency and thoroughness.

Learning from Incidents

The final and perhaps most crucial part of the incident management process is learning from the incidents. Every incident, regardless of its severity, holds lessons that can drive improvements in safety protocols and operational efficiencies.

Start by sharing findings from the investigation with all stakeholders, not just at the management level but across the entire organisation. This might be in the form of a safety bulletin, a workshop, or an update in training modules. The key is to communicate what changes will be made as a result of the incident to prevent its recurrence.

Implement the changes determined by the investigation. This could involve updates to safety protocols, changes in equipment, or modifications in workflows. It's essential that these changes are monitored to ensure they have the desired effect on safety and operations.

Lastly, consider a periodic review of past incidents and the effectiveness of subsequent changes. This could be part of an annual safety review. Such reviews can reveal patterns that weren't apparent initially and can show whether changes have led to improvements over time.

In conclusion, building a culture where incidents are seen as opportunities for learning and improvement rather than just failures requires a shift in perspective. By implementing robust systems for reporting, conducting thorough investigations, and ensuring learnings are integrated back into the operations, you can significantly enhance safety and efficiency in your logistics and warehousing operations. This proactive approach not only safeguards your employees but also boosts overall productivity and compliance, aligning with best practices in logistics and warehousing leadership.

Transparency and Accountability

Public Disclosure of Safety Performance

In the realm of logistics and warehousing, where operations are as complex as the machinery used, transparency isn't just a nice-to-have—it's an operational imperative. Let's talk about public disclosure of safety performance, a topic that might initially make you wince. After all, revealing internal data about safety incidents or near misses can feel like airing your dirty laundry. However, consider this: transparency encourages trust, and trust is the currency in today's business environment.

For starters, you might be wondering what exactly should be disclosed. The key is to focus on data that provides real insight into your safety practices and outcomes. This includes statistics on reported incidents, response times, and the effectiveness of safety measures implemented. It's not about showcasing perfection, but rather demonstrating a commitment to continuous improvement.

Think about using platforms that are accessible to your stakeholders—perhaps an annual safety report on your website or a section in your corporate social responsibility (CSR) reports. The format matters less than the content. Ensure that the data is presented in a clear, understandable manner, avoiding technical jargon that could alienate non-expert readers.

Moreover, consider the frequency of disclosure. Regular updates, perhaps on a quarterly basis, can keep safety at the forefront of everyone's minds and reassure stakeholders that it is being monitored continuously, not just when things go wrong.

Stakeholder Engagement

Engagement is not just about pushing information out; it's about dialogue. Engaging stakeholders in discussions about safety isn't just about ticking a box—it's about enhancing the effectiveness of your safety measures through diverse input and building a culture that values safety from the top down.

Start by identifying who your key stakeholders are. Aside from your employees, this group could include local community leaders, regulatory bodies, and even your customers. Each has a unique perspective on what safety means and why it's important, offering insights that can help shape better policies and practices.

How do you engage them effectively? Regular meetings and forums can be instrumental. These don't have to be formal events; even roundtable discussions or dedicated sessions during broader meetings can suffice. The goal is to create a space where stakeholders can voice their concerns, provide feedback, and suggest improvements.

Another effective tool is surveys. They can be particularly useful in gauging the effectiveness of your current safety protocols and identifying areas for improvement. Ensure that these surveys are easy to access and complete, and perhaps more crucially, that the feedback collected leads to actionable insights.

Building Trust Through Transparency

Lastly, let's dive into how transparency can be your ladder to building trust. In the logistics and warehousing sector, where the pace is unrelenting and the stakes are high, trust can make or break your operation. When stakeholders trust that you are managing risks effectively, they are more likely to show support when challenges arise.

Building this trust starts with consistency. If you say you are going to report safety performance quarterly, stick to that schedule. If you promise to implement changes based on stakeholder feedback, ensure those changes are visible and communicated. It's about walking the talk.

Transparency also involves admitting to mistakes—no operation is free from them. The key is how you handle these mistakes. Are they swept under the rug, or are they openly discussed and learned from? Opt for the latter. Show your stakeholders that every incident is a learning opportunity and that their safety and well-being are your top priorities.

Moreover, transparency should be seen not just as a regulatory requirement, but as an integral part of your business strategy. It should be woven into the fabric of your operations, from the onboarding of new employees to the execution of major projects. When transparency is treated as a core value rather than an obligation, it becomes a powerful tool for building trust and credibility.

In conclusion, embracing transparency and accountability in your safety practices is not just about compliance or public image—it's a strategic approach that can enhance operational efficiency, encourage innovation, and build a resilient business. By focusing on public disclosure, engaging stakeholders effectively, and leveraging transparency to build trust, you place your business on a solid foundation for long-term success.

RECAP AND ACTION ITEMS

You've just navigated through the crucial aspects of Health and Safety Metrics and Reporting in the logistics and warehousing sector. This knowledge is not just to empower you but to action change that enhances safety, streamlines operations, and solidifies your compliance framework.

Starting with Key Performance Indicators (KPIs), you've explored how selecting relevant metrics, tracking, and analysing them, and then reporting these findings to stakeholders, forms the backbone of effective health and safety management. Remember, the KPIs you choose should not only reflect your current safety performance but also drive improvements where they are most needed.

Moving to Incident Reporting and Investigation, the focus has been on establishing robust systems that ensure every incident is reported without fear of repercussion. Conducting effective investigations is not about assigning blame but about uncovering the root causes to prevent future occurrences. The learning derived from these incidents is a gold mine for preventing similar future events and should be integrated into your ongoing risk management strategy.

Lastly, the essence of Transparency and Accountability cannot be overstated. Public disclosure of safety performance might seem daunting but think of it as your organisation's safety CV to the world. Engaging stakeholders not just informs but also involves them in your journey towards a safer work environment. Building trust through transparency isn't just good ethics; it's good business.

ACTION STEPS:1. Audit Your Current KPIs: Review your existing safety KPIs to ensure they are still relevant to your operational reality. Adjust as necessary

2. Enhance Your Incident Reporting System: If your current incident reporting system is not up to scratch, now is the time to revamp it. Consider implementing anonymous reporting to encourage a more open reporting culture

3. Conduct a Training Review: Ensure that all employees are not only aware of the procedures for reporting and investigating incidents but are also trained in how to effectively execute these processes

4. Schedule Regular Safety Reviews: These should be with key stakeholders

to discuss current safety performance and any recent incidents. Use these meetings to encourage a culture of transparency and continuous improvement

5. Commit to Public Reporting: If you haven't already, start planning how to publicly disclose your safety performance. This could be through annual safety reports or a dedicated section on your company website.

Taking these steps will not only enhance your operational safety but will also position your organisation as a leader in safety management within the logistics and warehousing sector. Remember, every step you take towards improving safety is a step towards a more efficient and compliant operation.

10

Integrating Health and Safety with Business Strategy

"Health and safety are not just corporate responsibilities; they're strategic imperatives that harmonise with business success, ensuring prosperity for all stakeholders."
- Richard Branson

Aligning Safety with Business Objectives

In the fast-paced world of logistics and warehousing, aligning safety with business objectives isn't just a regulatory must-do; it's a strategic imperative that can differentiate your operations from the competition. Let's dive deep into how integrating safety can drive your business forward, enhance your return on investment (ROI), and streamline your strategic planning process.

Benefits of Integrating Safety

When you think about safety, the first benefits that likely spring to mind are reduced injury rates and compliance with health and safety regulations. While these are certainly critical, the advantages of integrating safety into your business strategy extend far beyond compliance.

Firstly, consider the impact on employee morale and retention. Workers in a safe and cared-for environment are more likely to stay with a company, reducing turnover and the costs associated with recruiting and training new staff. They're also more productive, as they aren't hampered by injuries or the fear of potential accidents.

Moreover, a strong safety record enhances your company's reputation. In today's socially conscious market, businesses are not only judged on their financial performance but also on their corporate responsibility. A reputation for safety can make your company a preferred partner for business and an attractive prospect for potential employees.

Finally, integrating safety can lead to innovation. Safe operations require you to constantly evaluate and improve your processes, which can lead to efficiencies that might not have been discovered otherwise. This proactive approach to safety can help you stay ahead of the curve in a competitive industry.

Strategic Planning

Incorporating safety into your strategic planning is not about ticking boxes. It's about embedding safety into every aspect of your operations and making it a core value rather than an afterthought.

Start with your corporate vision. How does safety align with the values and goals of your business? This alignment is crucial because it ensures that safety becomes a part of your company's DNA, woven into the fabric of every operational plan and strategy.

From there, consider your strategic objectives. Perhaps you aim to be the leader in your market or innovate your industry practices. How can safety drive these outcomes? For example, by reducing workplace accidents, you can cut down on lost workdays. Fewer injuries also mean fewer disruptions, allowing for smoother operations and improved productivity, which can accelerate your path to market leadership.

Another aspect of strategic planning is risk management. Every logistics and warehousing operation faces risks, from warehouse fires to supply chain disruptions. By integrating safety measures into your risk management strategies, you can mitigate these risks more effectively and ensure that your operation runs smoothly.

ROI on Safety Investments

Investing in safety might seem like an additional cost at first glance. However, the return on investment (ROI) on safety is compelling when you look at the broader picture.

First, calculate the direct costs of accidents and injuries in your workplace. These include medical expenses, damages to goods or machinery, and potential legal fees. Then, factor in the indirect costs, such as lost productivity, increased insurance premiums, and potential fines. The numbers start to add up quickly.

Now, compare these costs to the investment required for effective safety measures—things like training programs, safety equipment, and technology that enhances safe practices. Often, the cost of these safety investments is considerably lower than the costs associated with workplace accidents.

Moreover, investing in safety can yield significant savings in other areas. For instance, many insurers offer lower premiums to businesses that demonstrate robust safety practices. Additionally, maintaining a strong safety record can reduce downtime caused by accidents, keeping your operations running smoothly and efficiently.

Investing in safety technology can also provide substantial ROI. Technologies such as automated guided vehicles (AGVs) and warehouse management systems (WMS) not only improve safety but also enhance operational efficiency, leading to faster fulfillment times and higher customer satisfaction.

In conclusion, integrating safety with business objectives is not just about reducing risks—it's about creating a more engaged workforce, building a strong brand reputation, and driving operational efficiencies. By weaving safety into the fabric of your strategic planning and recognising its potential to provide significant ROI, you position your logistics or warehousing business not just to succeed, but to excel.

Budgeting for Safety

When it comes to ensuring the safety of your logistics and warehousing operations, budgeting isn't just a necessary evil; it's a strategic enabler. Let's dive into how you can allocate resources effectively, analyse the cost-benefit aspects, and manage safety expenditures without cutting corners or compromising the safety standards that keep your operations running smoothly.

Allocating Resources

First off, determining the financial commitment to safety is crucial. It's about investing, not spending. You need to think of safety-related expenditures as investments into the operational health and longevity of your business. But how do you decide what amount goes where?

Start with a risk assessment. Identifying potential risks and the severity of their consequences helps in prioritising the areas that need immediate attention and funding. For instance, if your warehouse involves high-level shelving, investing in fall protection systems and training might take precedence over other considerations.

Once risks are identified and prioritised, allocate your budget according to the potential impact of these risks. This doesn't mean throwing all your resources at the highest risks; even smaller risks can cascade into significant issues if not addressed. Allocate with a balance, ensuring that all potential risks are mitigated effectively.

Remember, resource allocation also includes manpower. Investing in a safety officer or a dedicated safety team depends on your operation's size and complexity. If outsourcing this role is more feasible, ensure the external expertise aligns with your business needs and safety culture.

Cost-Benefit Analysis

Every penny invested in safety needs to show its return, not necessarily immediately, but as a sustainable contribution to the business. Performing a cost-benefit analysis on safety investments can illuminate their worth.

Start by calculating potential losses from safety incidents, including downtime, legal fees, compensation, and reputational damage. Compare these costs against the investment required for preventive measures. Often, the potential losses due to safety incidents far outweigh the costs of prevention.

Let's say you're considering advanced ergonomics training for staff to reduce the incidence of musculoskeletal disorders, a common warehouse ailment. The upfront cost of such training might seem high, but weigh that against the cost of lost workdays, medical claims, and decreased productivity. The long-term savings can be substantial.

Moreover, there's an often-overlooked benefit: worker morale. Employees in a safe work environment are more engaged and productive. They're also less likely to leave, reducing turnover and the associated costs of hiring and training new staff.

Managing Safety Expenditures

Managing your safety budget effectively is as important as setting it. This involves regular review and adjustment, ensuring that your safety investment is responsive to any changes in your operational environment or in regulatory standards.

One approach is to incorporate safety into your broader financial management systems. Integrate safety-related metrics into your regular financial reporting.

This doesn't just help in tracking expenses but also in illustrating the impact of your safety investments on overall operational efficiency.

Technology can be a significant expenditure in your safety budget, but it's worth it. Investing in automation can reduce human error and the risk of accidents. For example, automated guided vehicles in a warehouse can reduce the need for forklift travel, one of the more common sources of accidents in warehousing environments.

Lastly, don't forget about the importance of contingency budgeting. Set aside a portion of your safety budget for unforeseen issues. This isn't about being pessimistic but prepared. In the dynamic field of logistics and warehousing, new safety challenges can emerge rapidly, and having the financial flexibility to tackle these head-on can be a game-changer.

In essence, budgeting for safety in logistics and warehousing isn't just about meeting legal standards or maintaining a status quo; it's a dynamic and integral part of your strategic business operations. It requires foresight, ongoing commitment, and a clear understanding of the interplay between cost and benefit. Done right, it not only protects but enhances your business operations, ensuring that safety and profitability go hand in hand.

Innovating Safety Practices

Collaborative Initiatives

In the ever-evolving field of logistics and warehousing, the push towards innovation isn't just about being better; it's about leading and setting benchmarks that redefine industry standards. A significant leap can be made by embracing collaborative initiatives. Think of it as harnessing collective wisdom—where minds from various facets of the industry converge to tackle safety from every angle.

You're already aware that logistics is not just about moving goods, but ensuring that each step is safe and efficient. By initiating partnerships, be they with other companies, governmental bodies, or educational institutions, you can tap into a broader spectrum of safety innovations. Imagine co-developing safety protocols with technology firms, or participating in government-led safety trials which offer early access to new regulatory insights and tools.

Collaboration can also extend to sharing data across companies and sectors to predict and mitigate risks more effectively. By collectively analysing accident data and safety breaches, you can identify patterns that might not be apparent in a smaller dataset. This big-picture view allows for more strategic interventions and the development of robust safety solutions that benefit everyone involved.

Moreover, these partnerships can lead to shared training programmes where the cost of development and execution is split among participants, reducing your individual investment but broadening the impact. Shared learning platforms can be particularly effective, as they allow employees from different companies to experience training scenarios that cover a wider range of potential incidents.

Leveraging Industry Trends

Keeping your finger on the pulse of new trends is crucial in maintaining a competitive edge. In the realm of safety, this means staying updated with technological advancements and integrating them into your operations. From wearables that monitor worker vitals and fatigue levels to AI-driven analytics for predicting potential hazard zones in a warehouse, technology offers a plethora of tools to enhance safety.

Drones, for instance, are becoming increasingly useful in large warehouse environments. They can be used to perform routine inventory checks in high, hard-to-reach places, reducing the need for human workers to engage in potentially hazardous tasks. Similarly, augmented reality (AR) can be utilised to train your staff in a safe, controlled virtual environment, simulating real-world scenarios without the real-world risks.

It's also worth paying attention to sustainability trends which often overlap with safety improvements. For example, cleaner, more organised warehouse spaces are not only good for the planet but also reduce accidents and injuries. Implementing energy-efficient lighting improves visibility, making it easier for your team to navigate safely around the workspace.

By integrating these technological trends into your safety protocols, you not only enhance worker safety but also improve overall efficiency and productivity—a win-win for any logistics operation.

Pioneering New Practices

As a leader in the logistics and warehousing sector, you have the power to set trends, not just follow them. Pioneering new safety practices can be a formidable task, but it's also an opportunity to establish your company as a front-runner in industry safety innovation.

Start by identifying unique challenges within your operations and brainstorm novel ways to address them. This could mean developing custom solutions where off-the-shelf products fail to meet your specific needs. For example, if standard safety barriers are too cumbersome for your fast-paced sorting areas, why not develop a more flexible, easy-to-move barrier system?

Engaging with frontline employees is crucial in this phase. They are the ones navigating these risks on a daily basis and can provide insights into what's working and what's not. This bottom-up approach not only ensures that your safety innovations are practical but also boosts employee morale by valuing their input.

Testing and refining these innovations requires a structured approach. Pilot them in controlled environments, gather feedback, and iterate quickly. Remember, the goal is not just to innovate for the sake of innovation, but to effectively enhance safety in a way that aligns with your operational needs and goals.

Finally, consider the broader implications of your pioneering practices. If successful, how can these be scaled or adapted for wider industry application? Sharing your findings and successes at industry conferences or in trade publications not only cements your status as an industry leader but also contributes to the collective goal of safer logistics operations globally.

By focusing on collaborative initiatives, leveraging industry trends, and pioneering new practices, you position your business not just to adapt to the evolving safety landscape, but to actively shape it. This proactive approach doesn't just mitigate risks—it enhances operational efficacy and sets you apart in a competitive industry

RECAP AND ACTION ITEMS

As you've journeyed through this chapter on integrating health and safety with your business strategy, you've gained insights into aligning safety with your business objectives, effectively budgeting for safety, and innovating safety practices. This is crucial in not only maintaining compliance but also in enhancing operational efficiency and employee morale in your logistics or warehousing operations.

Action Step1: Review and AlignTake a moment to review your current safety and business objectives. Are they in harmony? Start by identifying areas where safety protocols can directly contribute to achieving business goals, such as reducing workplace incidents to lower costs and improve productivity. Establish clear metrics to measure the impact of safety on business performance.

Action Step2: Budget SmartRe-examine your budget allocations towards safety measures. Are you investing enough to see a real return? Consider conducting a thorough cost-benefit analysis of your current and projected safety expenditures. Look into reallocating resources to more critical areas identified in the analysis that promise better compliance and safety outcomes.

Action Step3: encourage InnovationInitiate a brainstorming session with your team to explore innovative safety solutions. Think about how you can leverage new industry trends, like digital technology for real-time hazard monitoring or AI for accident prevention strategies. Encourage collaboration with other industry players or sectors to share best practices and new ideas.

Action Step4: Implement and EvaluateWith these strategies in place, move forward by implementing them systematically. Regularly evaluate the effectiveness of these new measures and be prepared to make adjustments as needed. This continuous improvement cycle will not only ensure safety compliance but also encourage a proactive culture of safety within your organisation.

By taking these steps, you will not only enhance the safety standards in your operations but also position your business as a forward-thinking leader in the logistics and warehousing sector. So, let's start putting these strategies into action today and pave the way for a safer and more efficient workplace.

11

Leveraging Health and Safety Consultancy for Strategic Advantage

"Safety and health can add value to your business, your job, and your life." - American Industrial Hygiene Association

The Value of Expertise

In the complex world of logistics and warehousing, the stakes are high and the margins often tighter than the lid on a well-sealed container. As a senior manager or director, your role isn't just about overseeing operations; it's about steering your company through the labyrinth of compliance, safety, and efficiency. This is where the value of expertise comes into sharp focus, particularly the expertise offered by accredited health and safety consultancies.

Benefits of Accredited Consultancies

Imagine you're at the helm of a ship. The sea is the ever-changing landscape of logistics and warehousing, and your ship is your company. Would you rather navigate these waters with or without a seasoned navigator? Accredited health and safety consultancies are like your navigators, equipped with the charts and tools to not only keep you afloat but to ensure you're sailing the most efficient route possible.

Engaging with accredited consultancies brings a swath of benefits. Firstly, they maintain a gold standard of service, validated by governing bodies that back their credentials. This isn't just paperwork; it's a promise of quality and reliability. For you, this means when you're audited or inspected, you're more likely to pass with flying colours—not because you've ticked boxes, but because your operations genuinely meet high standards.

Moreover, these consultancies are always on top of changes in legislation and technology. In the fast-paced world of logistics, new laws, and tech can roll out faster than new stock. Accredited consultants don't just help you keep up—they help you stay ahead. This proactive approach not only safeguards your business against compliance risks but also arms you with the knowledge to leverage new safety technologies and practices before your competitors do.

Qualifications and Accreditations

Let's delve a bit deeper into what these qualifications and accreditations mean for you and your company. In the UK, health and safety consultancies often boast accreditations, standards that are internationally recognised. These aren't just badges to polish and display in your lobby. They are indicative of a consultancy's ability to operate to certain standards that reduce workplace risks and enhance health and safety performance.

Employing a consultancy with such credentials also enhances your company's reputation. Think about it—when clients and partners see that your health and safety measures are guided by accredited experts, they see a business that values quality and responsibility. This can be a significant competitive edge in an industry where reputation can often dictate the opportunities that come your way.

Furthermore, the qualifications held by individual consultants matter. Certified professionals, whether NEBOSH, IOSH, or similar, bring a level of expertise that can be pivotal. These aren't just individuals who have read the rule book—they've mastered it, often bringing years of experience across various sectors. This depth of knowledge and perspective can be invaluable, particularly when unique or challenging situations arise.

Independent and Unbiased Advice

One of the most critical aspects of leveraging external expertise is the independence and unbiased nature of the advice you receive. Internal teams are invaluable, but there can be limitations due to company culture, internal politics, or simply the tunnel vision that comes with dealing with the same systems and processes day in, day out.

An independent consultancy comes with fresh eyes and zero baggage. Their sole objective is to ensure your operations are safe, compliant, and as efficient as possible. This can lead to insights and recommendations that might be overlooked internally, from small process tweaks to major strategic overhauls. And because these consultancies are impartial, you can trust that their advice is given with your company's best interests in mind, not hindered by internal agendas or resistance to change.

Moreover, this unbiased perspective is crucial when it comes to audits and assessments. These consultancies hold no punches—they tell it like it is, which although sometimes tough to hear, is exactly what's needed to ensure that your business isn't just meeting the minimum standards, but setting the benchmark for safety and compliance in the industry.

In conclusion, stepping up your game in logistics and warehousing isn't just about investing in the latest technologies or hiring more staff—it's about smart partnerships and leveraging external expertise. Accredited health and safety consultancies offer more than services; they provide a strategic advantage that can elevate your operations, safeguard your workforce, and position your business as a leader in a competitive market. As you navigate the complexities of the industry, think of these partnerships not as an expense but as an investment in the future of your logistics or warehousing enterprise.

Efficiency and Cost Savings

When weighing the potential benefits of partnering with a health and safety consultancy, efficiency and cost savings are often at the forefront of considerations. The drive for operational lean-ness without compromising safety can seem like a tightrope walk, but it's a balance that accredited consultancies are well-positioned to help you achieve. Let's dissect how these partnerships can streamline your health and safety processes, provide access to audited contractors, and deliver cost-effective solutions.

Streamlining Health and Safety Processes

Think of your current health and safety processes. How much of your day is consumed by ensuring these procedures are followed, monitoring outcomes, and updating protocols? It's likely a significant portion. Here's where a specialised consultancy can make a significant impact. By applying their expert knowledge, these consultancies can streamline your existing processes, eliminating redundancies and enhancing effectiveness.

Streamlining might involve integrating cutting-edge technology that automates regular monitoring and reporting, thus reducing the need for manual oversight. For instance, digital compliance tools can help track real-time data on warehouse operations, alerting you immediately to any deviations from set safety standards. This automation not only speeds up reaction times but also frees up your team to focus on core operational tasks.

Moreover, consultancies can help you implement a more coherent and unified approach to health and safety across various departments or even geographical locations. Consistency is key in reducing misunderstandings and errors, and a streamlined approach ensures that all team members are on the same page.

Access to Audited Contractors

One significant advantage of working with a top-tier health and safety consultancy is gaining access to a vetted pool of audited contractors. These contractors have undergone rigorous evaluations to ensure they meet specific health and safety standards, which is crucial in maintaining your compliance and operational integrity.

Think about the last time you had to contract out for services or temporary labour. The due diligence required to vet these contractors independently can be exhaustive—and it's compounded by the risk of overlooking critical compliance issues due to unfamiliarity or time constraints.

Health and safety consultancies typically maintain a roster of pre-approved contractors who have already been assessed for compliance with relevant health and safety regulations. This not only speeds up the contracting process but also mitigates risk, ensuring that everyone who steps onto your site is fully compliant with the latest health and safety standards. This access can be particularly beneficial during peaks in demand when you need to scale operations quickly and safely without the usual compliance headaches.

Cost-Effective Solutions

Implementing robust health and safety measures and maintaining compliance can be expensive, especially if you're aiming to stay ahead of the curve. However, the long-term financial benefits of engaging a health and safety consultancy can be substantial.

Firstly, consultancies can help you avoid the steep costs associated with non-compliance, including fines, legal fees, and the potential halt in operations.

These costs can quickly run into the hundreds of thousands, if not more, making the consultancy fees pale in comparison.

Secondly, by optimising your health and safety processes, consultancies help reduce the occurrence of workplace accidents and associated costs—ranging from medical bills and compensation payouts to lost workdays and reduced productivity. A safe work environment also boosts employee morale and retention, indirectly enhancing productivity and reducing recruitment and training costs.

Moreover, the cost-effectiveness of hiring a consultancy often extends beyond direct financial savings. For instance, consultancies can provide scalable solutions that grow with your business, ensuring you only pay for what you need when you need it. They can also offer flexible pricing models, such as subscriptions or fixed-fee services, which help you manage costs more predictively.

In the dynamic field of logistics and warehousing, where margins can be tight and the scope of operations vast, every efficiency gain and cost-saving measure counts. Leveraging the expertise of a health and safety consultancy not only supports compliance but also enhances overall operational resilience. This strategic partnership allows you to focus on core business activities, secure in the knowledge that your health and safety practices are both cost-effective and robust, tailored to meet both current needs and future challenges.

Enhancing Management Focus

Delegating Compliance Responsibilities

Let's face it, the complexity and sheer volume of health and safety regulations can be daunting. As a senior manager or director, your day is already packed with critical decisions, strategy meetings, and leadership responsibilities. Now, imagine offloading the weighty compliance tasks to a team of seasoned experts. This isn't just about clearing your plate; it's about utilising your focus where it counts.

By engaging a health and safety consultancy, you delegate these specialised responsibilities to professionals who live and breathe regulatory compliance. They're in the loop on the latest legislations and know precisely how to tailor their knowledge to benefit your specific operations. This isn't merely outsourcing; it's strategic empowerment, giving you the freedom to focus on core business activities while experts handle the complexities of compliance.

This delegation does wonders for your mental space and organisational efficiency. Think about it: no more diving into the minutiae of legislation, no more scrambling to keep up with the latest Health and Safety Executive (HSE) guidelines. Instead, you get distilled insights and actionable advice, all while ensuring your company remains on the right side of the law. It's about working smarter, not harder, and letting specialist knowledge streamline the path to compliance.

Time Management for Senior Managers

Efficient time management is pivotal in your role. Every minute saved from one task is an extra minute invested in another, potentially adding much more value. Health and safety consultancy can play a significant role in optimising how your time is spent. By entrusting these critical yet time-consuming tasks to experts, you reclaim hours in your week, hours that can be redirected towards strategic thinking and leadership.

Consultancies can help systematise the health and safety processes, from risk assessments to training programmes, thereby reducing the frequency and length of the meetings you need to attend on these issues. Regular updates and reports can be streamlined into concise briefs that allow you to grasp the essentials at a glance, without needing to get bogged down in details.

Moreover, consultants can act as your strategic partners, anticipating needs and preparing solutions before you even have to ask. This proactive approach not only saves time but also enhances your capability to make informed, timely decisions in other areas of your operations.

Project Delivery by Experts

Now, onto the tangible outputs of engaging a health and safety consultancy—project delivery. When you have new initiatives or need to overhaul existing systems, these projects often require detailed safety assessments and bespoke solutions. Here's where the real value of hiring experts becomes evident. Consultants bring a wealth of experience from working across various industries and can draw on best practices that have been proven effective elsewhere.

Their expertise enables them to foresee potential pitfalls and bottlenecks, advising on the most efficient execution strategies. This means projects are not only completed with a higher standard of safety compliance but are also more likely to be delivered on schedule and within budget. In essence, you're not just ensuring that projects tick regulatory boxes; you're enhancing their overall success and ROI.

Furthermore, consultants can manage these projects end-to-end. From initial assessments and planning through to implementation and final review, having a dedicated team focused solely on health and safety can significantly enhance the quality and outcomes of your projects. This level of management not only supports compliance but also drives innovation in safety practices, setting new benchmarks within your operations.

Each of these elements—delegating compliance responsibilities, mastering time management, and expert project delivery—converge to significantly enhance your managerial focus. In a role where every decision can influence the direction of your organisation, having the mental clarity and time to concentrate on what really matters can be your strategic advantage. With the support of a health and safety consultancy, you're not just meeting standards; you're setting them, ensuring your operations are not only compliant but also competitively distinguished in the logistics and warehousing industry.

RECAP AND ACTION ITEMS

As we've explored, leveraging health and safety consultancy not only bolsters your compliance strategies but also positions your logistics or warehousing operations for enhanced efficiency and strategic advantage. By engaging with accredited consultancies, you reap the benefits of expert, unbiased advice tailored to the unique needs of your sector. This is about not just meeting regulatory standards but exceeding them, ensuring that your operations are not just safe but also optimally effective.

Let's translate these insights into concrete actions:

1. Evaluate Your Current Health and Safety Protocols: Start by assessing how your current safety and compliance measures stack up. Identify areas where gaps exist or improvements are needed. This initial audit will help you understand the baseline from which you can improve.

2. Select an Accredited Consultancy: Choose a consultancy with the relevant accreditations and a proven track record in the logistics and warehousing industry. Look for consultants who hold qualifications that are recognised nationally and internationally, ensuring they bring a compliant and informed perspective to your operations.

3. Implement Independent Reviews: Once you have your consultancy in place, task them with conducting an independent review of your current practices. Their unbiased perspective can unveil hidden inefficiencies or overlooked risks that could be silently draining your resources or posing potential hazards.

4. Focus on Streamlining Processes: Work with your consultants to stream-

line your health and safety processes. This might involve integrating new technologies or simplifying procedures to reduce time and financial costs, all while maintaining a high standard of safety.

5. Delegate for Enhanced Focus: Utilise consultancy services to delegate compliance responsibilities. This enables you and your senior management team to focus more on core business strategies and less on the intricacies of compliance, which can be thoroughly managed by your chosen experts.

6. Review Contractor Arrangements: Ensure that your consultancy helps you access audited and vetted contractors. This step is crucial for maintaining a supply chain that adheres to your safety and efficiency standards.

7. Monitor and Adjust Regularly: Finally, establish a routine of regular check-ins with your consultancy. Use these meetings to review the effectiveness of implemented changes, adapt strategies as necessary, and continue pushing for operational excellence.

By following these steps, you can transform health and safety from a compliance necessity into a strategic asset that drives business success. Remember, the goal here is not just to survive inspections but to thrive in a competitive market by ensuring safety, efficiency, and compliance are at the heart of your operations.

12

Examples from the Field: Success Stories in Health and Safety Consultancy

"Safety is something that happens between your ears, not something you hold in your hands." - Jeff Cooper

In this chapter, we delve into the specific cases where our consultancy has made a significant impact on various organisations. These real-world examples illustrate the diverse challenges we've tackled and the tailored solutions we've provided to ensure compliance, safety, and efficiency.

Astral Control Services Ltd

Astral Control Services Ltd faced a critical need to update their health and safety policy. Our approach began with a comprehensive review of their existing policies. This review was meticulous, focusing on identifying gaps and areas for improvement. We aimed to align their procedures with the latest regulatory standards and best practices, ensuring that the company not only met but exceeded industry requirements.

Our next step involved a series of training sessions designed to educate their staff about the new policies. These sessions were interactive and practical, ensuring that employees understood the changes and knew how to implement them in their daily operations. The training included practical examples and hands-on activities, which were crucial in embedding the new practices into their routine. The result was a robust health and safety framework that not only enhanced compliance but also promoted a culture of safety within the organisation. Employees felt more confident and engaged, understanding that their well-being was a top priority.

ABI Equipment

ABI Equipment, one of our long-term partners, benefits from our continuous support and expertise. Our services for ABI Equipment include regular reviews and updates of their risk assessments and Control of Substances Hazardous to Health (COSHH) assessments. This ongoing process ensures that their health and safety measures remain current and effective.

Our bespoke advice is tailored to address specific operational hazards unique to ABI Equipment. For instance, we identified particular risks associated with their heavy machinery operations and provided targeted solutions to mitigate these risks. We also delivered hands-on manual handling training to their workforce. This training was not merely a tick-box exercise; it was designed to impart practical skills that employees could apply in their daily tasks. The result was a significant reduction in manual handling injuries and an overall improvement in workplace safety. Employees appreciated the practical nature of the training, which empowered them to handle materials more safely and efficiently.

Quality Fruit & Veg Limited

Quality Fruit & Veg Limited required a comprehensive health and safety site inspection. Our team conducted an exhaustive evaluation of their facilities, meticulously identifying potential hazards and ensuring that their safety practices met industry standards. This inspection covered various aspects of their operations, from storage and handling of produce to employee welfare facilities.

We provided a detailed report with actionable recommendations aimed at enhancing their safety protocols. These recommendations included practical steps to improve ventilation in storage areas, better handling procedures for heavy crates, and enhanced training for staff on emergency procedures. Implementing these recommendations has been instrumental in helping Quality Fruit & Veg Limited maintain compliance with health and safety regulations. The result was a safer working environment where employees felt more secure, and management had a clear roadmap for maintaining high safety standards.

Beanworks Coffee Roasters

Beanworks Coffee Roasters benefits from our ongoing consultancy services as a retained client. Our initial engagement involved a thorough review and update of their risk and COSHH assessments. This process was crucial in ensuring that their health and safety measures reflected current operational realities and regulatory changes.

We provided strategic advice and assisted in implementing a robust health and safety management system. This system was designed to integrate seamlessly into their daily operations, promoting a culture of safety and compliance across the organisation. One of the key components of this system was the introduction of regular safety audits and employee feedback mechanisms. These measures helped Beanworks Coffee Roasters continuously monitor and improve their safety practices. The result was a significant reduction in workplace incidents and a heightened awareness of health and safety among employees. The management team also benefited from clear and actionable insights, which helped them make informed decisions to enhance workplace safety.

Cinch Self Storage

Our consultancy conducted a detailed health and safety site inspection for Cinch Self Storage. This involved a meticulous examination of their storage facilities, identification of potential risks, and evaluation of existing safety measures. Our team spent several days on-site, observing operations, interviewing staff, and reviewing documentation.

The outcome was a comprehensive report with practical recommendations to enhance their health and safety practices. These recommendations included improvements in fire safety measures, better organisation of storage areas to prevent accidents, and enhanced training for staff on emergency procedures. Implementing these recommendations has helped Cinch Self Storage provide a safer environment for both employees and customers. The management team appreciated the thoroughness of our inspection and the practicality of our recommendations, which were easy to implement and had a tangible impact on safety.

Flying Logistics

For Flying Logistics, we conducted an in-depth health and safety site inspection and developed comprehensive risk assessments tailored to their specific operational needs. Our assessment encompassed all facets of their logistics processes, identifying potential hazards and recommending preventive measures.

We focused on areas such as warehouse operations, vehicle safety, and employee training. Our recommendations included practical steps to improve traffic management within the warehouse, better ergonomic practices for handling heavy loads, and enhanced safety protocols for vehicle operations. This proactive approach enabled Flying Logistics to create a safer working environment, significantly enhancing their overall safety performance. Employees felt more secure, and the management team gained valuable insights into improving operational safety.

G2 Energy Limited

Our consultancy performed a detailed health and safety site inspection for G2 Energy Limited, with a particular focus on lone working conditions. Lone working presents unique challenges, and our team was tasked with evaluating the associated risks and providing tailored recommendations to enhance safety.

We conducted a thorough assessment of their lone working practices, including reviewing existing safety measures, interviewing employees, and evaluating communication systems. Our recommendations included the implementation of advanced monitoring and communication systems, enhanced training for lone workers, and the introduction of regular check-ins to ensure employee safety. Our interventions ensured that lone workers had the necessary support and safety measures in place to carry out their tasks securely. The result was a safer working environment where lone workers felt supported and management had a clear strategy for managing lone working risks.

Conclusion

These examples highlight how partnering with a health and safety consultancy can provide tailored solutions, ensuring that your business remains compliant, efficient, and safe. Our consultancy takes pride in delivering practical, effective, and sustainable health and safety solutions. By addressing specific challenges and providing ongoing support, we help organisations create safer work environments and encourage a culture of safety and compliance. Whether it's updating policies, conducting thorough site inspections, or providing hands-on training, our commitment to excellence in health and safety consultancy is unwavering.

13

Acorn Compliance Antidote©

The UK's Only Fully Documented and Systemised Health and Safety Management Process

We help you to become fully compliant which prevents accidents, prosecution and fines.

Remove Your Health and Safety Problems Today.

How Can the Process And System Help You?

You see, the thing is in today's busy world most people have 101 things already on their plate and compliance and health and safety is piled on and often overlooked. This has become apparent to all those people and businesses that have been fined and prosecuted for health and safety failings.

Its not through a lack of wanting to make sure people are safe from the dangers its often not having the time or knowledge required to A) Stop people being injured and B) Having the time to implement everything.

Compliance and health and safety is a minefield and can be a painful process to try and implement yourself. This is why we exist as a business to help those that really do want to get everything straight and remove the health safety and compliance problem.

This is why we have invented the Acorn Compliance Antidote©.

The Acorn Compliance Antidote is an A - Z process that takes you from non-compliance through to full compliance so that you are fully legal in line with the Governments rules, regulations and laws.

After completing the 5 stage process you will no longer have to worry about your health and safety management or what to do when you get visits from the Health and Safety Executive.

The process is fully laid out to follow in a step by step and pragmatic manner with your consultant forging the way for you.

There are 5 stages to go through which ensures that all bases are covered and that all boxes are ticked.

But this is no box ticking exercise there is lots of work to be completed but the good news is that your consultant will be doing the majority of the work.

They will just need your valuable input to gather information agree a process and then assist when rolling the completed management process to your staff and teams.

You can take back control of your day to day you can get on with the things you want to do knowing that health and safety is no longer an issue for you

How Do I Know If I Need Help?

Only you can truly know the answer to that question. Most people do have doubts over systems and fears that their contractors are not doing things properly. Some have even identified flaws in processes but don't know how to solve the issues.

A lot of people also inherit health and safety as part of their job but they have never been trained and just do not know where to begin. You may be an expert but don't have the time to deal with everything as it should be dealt with.

Where do you fit on this scale?

Unconscious — unaware of the skills, knowledge and proficiency for health and safety management

Conscious — aware of the skills and knowledge required but not yet proficient

Competent — able to manage health and safety but only with time and effort

Auto Competence — health and safety management is performed automatically

Health and Safety Consequence Rating

Risk of accidents, prosecution and fines

Avoid prosecution, saves your reputation and keeps people safe

What Are The Stages Of The Asbestos Antidote?

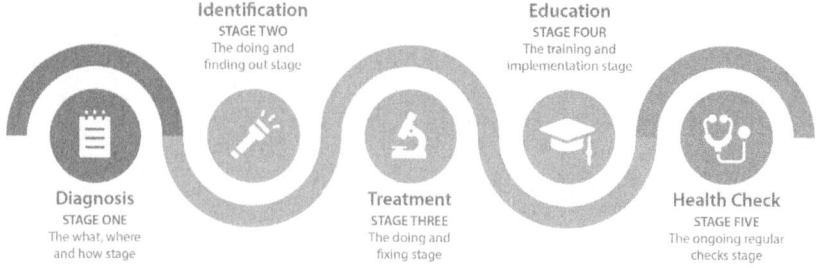

How Can the Process and System Help You?

Stage 1 – Diagnosis

- About You
- About Us
- Audit
- Process
- Results

Why?

For true diagnosis, you need to take stock of your current asbestos management position. You need to be certain that everything is in place and that everything is up to date which is a difficult thing to do with the ever changing regulations. Diagnosis will really and truly identify where the problems lay. Sometimes they're obvious ones that are on the surface and easy to fix. However, like any good doctor they identify issues that are on the surface as well as ones that you didn't even know existed. Now, what most people can the see is when they have got their diagnosis, they can finally see exactly what's going on.

How?

The diagnosis stage is a consultative process for both of us, you need to know about us and make sure we're a good fit for your company and likewise we need to ensure that we're a good fit for you and we can meet your exact needs. We carry out an audit of where you are at looking through what you have and discussing everything with you. This then reveals the process for the next steps. As every client is different and at different stages with their health and safety the results are presented in a bespoke report to you which we fully explain. You can take back control of your day to day, you can get on with the things you want to do knowing that the health and safety issue is no longer an issue for you.

Stage 2 – Identification

- Programme
- Identify
- Record
- Assess
- H&S Plan

Why?

To identify is to know. At the end of this stage you will have cast iron evidence of where you are at and what the health and safety in your properties looks like. This removes uncertainty and lets you finally see and identify the issues that you face, once and for all. This lays the foundations of health and safety management and starts to form the basis of your health and safety plan.

How?

The identification stage is where we programme in what initial site work needs to be carried out so that we can fully identify the health and safety risks. This is scheduled into a programme of works that fits around how your business operates so that we can achieve the highest hit rate in the shortest period of time. This information then is processed and is added to formulate your bespoke health and safety plan. This again is a consultative process between both of us, we will already have some idea on how your business operates from completing stage one plus the site work we have completed at stage two. This information is all taken into consideration when your health and safety plan is produced, this is then reviewed and agreed by you so that you know it is totally fit for purpose and so that you know everything has been covered.

Stage 3 – Treatment

- Consult
- Specification
- Tender & review
- Programme
- Execution

Why?

Treatment is the fixing stage. Depending on whats been identified at stage two depends how in depth this stage is. If there are a lot of items that need to be fixed such as asbestos or fire safety then this is the stage that its completed. Fixing the issues through projects can be a complicated process and they can easily go pear shaped. The trouble is when most people go about treatment is they look at using outside contractors. And outside contractors mess the whole thing up especially when you end up with a dodgy contractor. Because they don't really care, they provide you with inexperienced people and they botch the whole thing up which leaves you worse off than when you started.

How?

The treatment stage is where we consult with you the findings from stage two and agree a way forward. We will then produce bespoke specifications for any required works and formally tender these to approved contractors. Once the tender process has been completed, we will present the results and agree an appropriate timescale for the works and how these will be carried out. These works are then managed to ensure they are completed to your satisfaction and are carried out safely. This is where we also carry out regular checks to ensure that everything is completed properly.

Stage 4 – Education

- Awareness
- Health and Safety Training
- Database

Why?

Education is about spreading the word about "the dreaded health and safety" but spreading it the right way. This is so that you can get the team on side, actively helping and assisting you with health and safety management and stopping issues before they even arise. The worrying reality being if this stage is handled badly you can end up with a workforce that's scared, won't do their job and will become a massive thorn in your side. When handled correctly and a system is followed education can be a secret weapon in managing health and safety.

How?

Stage 4 is all about execution and roll out of all of the processes we have worked on thus far. All staff that require training will be given bespoke training. This is completed with limited downtime and gives the ability for any questions to be answered which reassures people and brings them on board collectively.

Stage 5 – Health Check

- Health and Safety Audit
- Inspection's / Servicing
- Planned Works

Why?

Health checks are really important because this is where you can identify what is working and what is not. You need to check the health and safety systems and processes in place are working appropriately. Once checked you need to update all of the paperwork, the reports, the policies the risk assessments etc so that you stay on the right side of the law. The problem is this is where most people fail, it's a massive task and a time consuming one at that. You also need to ensure that all of your obligations are met for any servicing or inspections of equipment is carried out.

How?

Stage five is a completeness in itself but one that then continues on year after year. The health and safety plan will be audited to ensure it is still fit for purpose and it is still working, servicing or inspections will take place to ensure that everything is in shape. This stage will also look at any planned works for the year and these will be planned in to ensure that the elements within stages two and three are followed. This essentially ensures that everything is working and is planned and stays on track as per your overall plan.

Still Looking to Remove Your Problems?

CLAIM YOUR FREE STRATEGY SESSION
PROTECT YOU AND YOUR BUSINESS NOW

Claim your no obligation free 20 minute strategy session now and get your custom Asbestos Health and Safety Blueprint, FREE!!

Send an email to **info@acornhealthandsafety.co.uk** and quote FREE STRATEGY SESSION

Or Pick up the phone and speak to Zeynep on 01604 930380

We're offering you a 20 minute strategy session where we'll discuss your goals and challenges and draw up a H&S Blueprint for you for free.

You will be speaking with one of our experienced Consultants.

Embracing The Future: a Call to Action for Continued Safety Excellence

In the rapidly evolving world of logistics, the paramount importance of safety and risk management cannot be understated. The journey through this book has equipped you with the core principles and innovative strategies needed to navigate the complexities of health and safety within the logistics sector. Now, as we draw this discussion to a close, the tools and knowledge you've acquired are your empowerment. They serve not just as a guide but as a catalyst for transformation within your organisation.

The landscape of logistics is one of unceasing change. Technology advances, regulatory landscapes shift, and operational demands grow increasingly complex. In such an environment, complacency can be the biggest threat to safety. Therefore, the commitment to continuous improvement and proactive risk management is crucial. It's not just about adhering to regulations; it's about surpassing them, setting new standards, and leading by example in your industry.

You have explored various facets of safety and risk management: from the essentials of health and safety law to the integration of cutting-edge technological innovations. Each element discussed is a piece of the puzzle, integral to constructing a robust safety culture that permeates every level of your organisation. But knowledge alone isn't enough—it's the application of this knowledge that will drive real change.

Implementing strategies requires a steadfast dedication and a clear vision.

It demands leadership that is both courageous and compassionate, capable of steering their teams through the complexities of modern logistics with an unwavering focus on safety and efficiency. As you move forward, remember that the journey towards safety excellence is continuous. Every day presents new challenges and opportunities for improvement.

Reflect on the safety within your organisation. Is it merely about compliance, or is it about setting benchmarks? Does it empower every employee to act as a custodian of their own safety and that of their colleagues? Cultivating a culture that prioritises safety above all else is not achieved overnight. It requires persistence, leadership, and most importantly, a collective effort.

Moreover, the role of technology in enhancing safety cannot be overlooked. As you have seen, innovations are not just tools but partners in achieving safety objectives. They provide insights that were previously unattainable, enabling you to predict risks and mitigate them before they manifest into incidents. Embrace these technologies, understand them deeply, and integrate them into your safety protocols. Let them serve you in creating an environment that prioritises human life and quality of service alike.

As you stand at this juncture, ready to apply what you've learned, remember that the path ahead is not one you need to walk alone. Collaboration and professional guidance are key in navigating the complexities of safety in logistics. Whether it's refining your existing protocols, training your team, or integrating new technologies, expert advice can provide the clarity and direction needed to enhance your safety strategies effectively.

If you find yourself seeking further expertise to elevate your safety standards or to discuss the unique challenges your organisation faces, do not hesitate to reach out. Visit www.acornhealthandsafety.co.uk to connect with professionals who can provide tailored advice and solutions. This is your opportunity to not only protect but to propel your organisation forward with enhanced safety measures and risk management strategies.

In closing, let this book not merely be a resource but a beginning. Let it inspire you to take proactive steps towards safety excellence. The principles and practices discussed here are your foundation. Build upon them, challenge them, and refine them as you forge your path forward in the logistics sector.

Safety is not a destination but a journey – one that requires diligence, innovation, and an unwavering commitment to continuous improvement. As you turn each page and implement the strategies, keep your eyes on the horizon, knowing that with each step, you are contributing to a safer, more efficient, and more sustainable future.

Thank you for joining me on this journey. Let's continue it together, reach out and let's make safety a cornerstone of your success.

Other Titles Available From Amazon

Asbestos The Dark Arts

Fear and Loathing of Health & Safety

Legionella The Dark Arts

Fire Risk The Dark Arts

Still Looking to Remove Your Problems?

Do you want help instead of going it alone?
Are you sure you're legally compliant?

Send an email to **info@acornhealthandsafety.co.uk** and quote
FREE STRATEGY SESSION

Or Pick up the phone and speak to Zeynep on 01604 930380

Call or email today for your free 20 minute strategy session

Printed in Great Britain
by Amazon